OUR ORDINARY LIVES HOLD AN EXTRAORDINARY PURPOSE

JERAD P. BISSON

outskirts press

Our Ordinary Lives Hold an Extraordinary Purpose

v2.0

Outskirts Press, Inc.
http://www.outskirtspress.com

ISBN: 978-1-4787-9158-4

PRINTED IN THE UNITED STATES OF AMERICA

In honor of
Jesus
Mary
Saint Michael
and my
guardian angel
who pushed me to complete this good work

Special thanks to my fiancée Jasmine Ramirez
my mother Janis Bisson
my father Peter Bisson
and
Saint Bonaventure Parish
for all the love and
support they all gave
me during this
journey.

Table of Contents

Table of Contents

Introduction

Most people live a rather ordinary life. many of us are not professional athletes or movie stars, and the truth is none of us have to be, to be significant. In fact, the insignificant are the ones that God loves to use the most, the ones he chooses to accomplish some of the most amazing tasks throughout history. From Saint Joan of Arc to Saint Joseph or all the apostles, every person who has ever been called by God was ordinary. That's because God uses the foolish things of this world to shame the wise, the weak to shame the strong (1 Corinthians 1:27 RSV Catholic edition). When the ordinary achieve great accomplishments, they won't boast; instead they will give the glory to God.

If you're an average person, consider yourself blessed because God has a plan for your life from beginning to end. Plans for welfare and not for evil, to give you a future and a hope. (Jeremiah 29:11 RSV Catholic Edition). So, let us embark on a journey to find out what those plans are. This book is a guide to help aid you in this quest. You have always seen yourself for who you are. Now it's time that you see yourself through the eyes of God to see yourself as the person you were always meant to be. Who are we to say who we are? A gift is something that is given to us that we did nothing to earn, and our lives were given to us freely without us earning a single beat of our hearts. Therefore, our very lives are a gift meant for a specific purpose. That is why we must ask the one who gave us this gift what its purpose is.

God will never give you anything that you can't handle. Rather, he will prepare you and groom you for what tasks lie ahead. If there is anything that you are lacking, he will compensate in grace. If you follow all the steps in this book and come to the Lord in faith, honesty, and diligence, there is nothing that you can't accomplish. God's plan is to live an adventure through your life. When we allow him to guide us in his will and let him tell our story, instead of us telling our own story, we can rest assured that the Lord will use us for great and extraordinary work that we may bear fruit, fruit that will last. So that whatever we ask God the Father in the name of Jesus he will give it to us (John 15:16 RSV Catholic edition). Most of your life you have been the judge of many things. It's time to let God be the judge for you, to help guide you, to help strengthen you, to help enrich you, and to prepare you for a mission so you may walk with him and so he may lead you to everlasting life.

Ordinary People

HAVE YOU EVER felt, more often than not, as if your life is meaningless or ordinary? If so, there's good news! We have a loving creator, who loves to take the lowly and put them on high, (Ezekiel 21:26 RSV Catholic Edition). I love reminding people that throughout history God has always chosen the weak, insignificant, ordinary people to do incredible tasks for him (Corinthians 1:27 RSV Catholic Edition). Many of us lead seemingly insignificant lives. That's exactly the kind of person God uses. In fact, many of the saints were common people. All saints didn't start out as priests or nuns. Most of them were ordinary people like you and me before God asked them to do something. I'm sure when they realized that God was interested in them and they had an idea of what God wanted them to do, they probably were shocked that God chose them to do it.

My point is don't be surprised if someday God asks you to do some good works for him. I want you to realize that we are all called to serve God. We are all called to be holy. We are all his people, especially if you lead an ordinary life. Take me. I have terrible handwriting. I don't space my words, everything gets jumbled up, and nobody can read what I wrote, yet here I am writing a book. Many of us have flaws that we may think are our weaknesses. God sees these weaknesses as opportunities: to show the world and you what great things ordinary people can accomplish when they put their trust and faith in him (Matthew 17:20 RSV Catholic Edition); to show the people he chooses exactly what they're capable of, as well as using them as an example for others; and to see that we can do anything when we believe and rely on his help.

Let's look at the life of Saint Joseph. As church tradition states, it was the time of year when the Jewish temple arranged marriages. Mary was a young girl who was consecrated to God and did not wish to marry. Joseph also was a righteous man of God who was not seeking to marry either. Nevertheless, the priest had a dream that he would collect all the eligible men's staffs together and the staff of the man whom the priest was to betroth to Mary would reveal itself to him. The priest collected all the staffs, and the staff that belonged to Joseph bloomed with flowers. When Joseph saw his staff, which he held and walked with every day, blooming with flowers, he became confused and amazed that God wanted him to get married. He was a devout man of God. He wasn't wealthy; he worked with his hands as an ordinary carpenter. Yet God still chose him. Not much is said about Saint Joseph in the Bible. We do know that he raised Jesus and taught him about the Jewish faith, work ethic, and how to be a man.

So here we have an ordinary man who today the world knows, who in the order of saints is at the right hand of our Blessed Mother. He is known to many and the church as the scourge of the demons, as well as the sacred saint of fathers and laborers. Saint Joseph was not a priest or rabbi or Levite for that matter. He was just a devout man of God who wished to serve him faithfully. and he did, just not in the way he was expecting. Just like everyone else who has ever been called to serve the Lord.

I'm sure many of us, if asked right now, could name our strengths and our weaknesses. I'm pretty sure you avoid your weaknesses more than your strengths because your strengths are what you're good at. when asked to do something that involves our weaknesses however, we try to avoid it. We think we can't do it. But the Lord says that with him we can do anything! Isaiah 40:31 RSV Catholic Edition says, "But they who wait for the Lord shall renew their strength. They shall mount up with wings like eagles they shall run and not be weary, they shall walk and not be faint." Such inspiring and truthful words from the prophet Isaiah. We ordinary Christians need encouragement from words like these to remind us who we serve, who we are, and who God says we can be, for he created us for him and for his purposes. We are each made with the gifts of his choosing.1Peter 4:10 RSV Catholic edition states, "As each has received a gift, employ it for one another, as good stewards of God's varied grace." Romans 12:06-8 RSV Catholic Edition states, "Having gifts that differ according to the grace given to us, let us use them: if prophecy, in proportion to our faith; if service, in our serving; he who teaches, in his teaching; he who exhorts in his exhortation; he who contributes in his liberality; he who gives aid, with zeal; he who does acts of mercy, with cheerfulness." So, we have to ask ourselves, are we using our gifts wisely to help others in accordance with our faith? Do we even know what our gifts are? Ask yourself, "What are my strengths? What are my weaknesses?" Have you attempted to see if there is anything hidden in your weaknesses? All my life I have avoided writing; I always thought it was something that I just was not good at. Is there anything in your life that you see as a weakness that might not be? For me it was writing; what's yours?

Recap: God chooses insignificant people to do incredible tasks for him. If you feel like your life is meaningless, would you let Jesus in to make it meaningful?

Step 1: Identify your strengths and weaknesses. Explore your weaknesses and see if there is a gift hiding that you may have missed all your life. Make a list of your strengths and weaknesses to give you a better perspective on what your gifts may be. Use that gift to help others, to show the world that all things are possible with God.

Sign of the cross
Almighty and ever living God, by your goodness and merciful desire for the salvation of all mankind, I beseech thee to reveal to me my true spiritual gifts, which are hidden from me, so that I may use them for my mission. I promise to use whatever gift you reveal to me to help my community and to love my neighbor.

In Jesus's name, amen.

Strengths	Weaknesses

Adam, Where Are You?

TO FIND OUT how God wants to use us, we must let Jesus prepare us for our mission. All the spiritual gifts God has created for each of us are intended for us to use to accomplish our purpose (Romans 12:06 RSV Catholic Edition). Many of us, whether we went to catechism when we were children or didn't have parents who were devout in the faith, may have a failed misconception of how sin affects us and our relationship with God. A *mortal sin* is a gravely wrongful act, which can lead to eternal damnation if a person is not absolved of this sin before death. Its quality is such that it leads to a separation from God's saving grace.

Now, before I get into the meat and potatoes of this chapter, I want you to know that I believe that nothing can separate us from the love of God. He came and died for us while all of us were in the filth of our sin. The apostle Paul also believed this. In Romans 8:38–39 RSV Catholic Edition, he wrote, "For I am sure that neither death, nor life, nor angels nor principalities, nor things present nor things to come, nor powers, nor height nor depth, nor anything else in all creation, will separate us from the love of God in Christ Jesus our Lord." The separation I speak of in this chapter is the separation of your relationship with God—your state of grace, if you will, of the relationship between God and you.

Let's look at the book of Genesis. In the beginning, God created Adam. He gave Adam the honor of naming all the birds of the air and the beasts of the earth and the sea that God had created. God noticed that Adam was not content with being alone when God left the garden. So, God put Adam in a deep sleep and removed one of his ribs. From this rib, he created Eve (Genesis 2:22 RSV Catholic Edition). Adam was on good terms with God. God gave Adam everything that he needed. In an equivalent way, when we are in a state of grace with the Lord, he will give us everything that we need for our mission as well. When we are not on good terms with God, he will give us everything that we need to put us back in a right relationship with him again if we present ourselves humbly before him. For example, if someone is going to reconciliation regularly, has a holy hour every day for prayer and reading the Bible or other forms of spiritual books, is putting the teachings of Jesus into action, is trusting in the intercession of our Blessed Mother, and is strongly committed to amending his or her life, this person is ready for direction from our merciful creator. This person has been receiving guidance and instruction by means of the Holy Spirit, which has brought him or her to communing with God on a regular basis. This person can recognize when Jesus asks him or her to do something. When someone is not in a state of grace, this person is not prepared for his or her mission just yet. Always remember, Jesus wants us to come to him the way that we are so he can fix what is broken within us, putting us in an appropriate condition to accomplish our purpose. Our God is a God of healing, no matter how big or how small our problems are. He is always willing to help us overcome adversities.

Let's look at Mark 5:12 RSV Catholic Edition, the story of the possessed man who lived in the tombs. When he came to

Jesus, he was possessed by demons and was separated from a relationship with God. This man was suffering severely, yet still he came to Jesus in the state that he was in. Jesus then cast the demons out from him. The man, now in the right state of mind, begged Jesus to let him go with him and his disciples on his journey. Jesus did not permit him to go with them. Instead he told him, "Go home to your friends and tell them how much the Lord has done for you and how he has had mercy on you" (Mark 5:19 RSV Catholic Edition). So, the man did as Jesus asked, and all who knew the man were amazed. You see, the man didn't wait until he was perfect to come to Jesus. He came to him broken and imperfect so God could fix him, healing him and giving him peace. Now the man was eager and ready to serve God. Now the man was ready for his mission, and Jesus gave it to him.

In a comparable way, we too must come to Jesus the way that we are to form a relationship with him, so he may fix what is broken within us and so we may reconnect ourselves to him and open a line of communication between him and us. Notice that the possessed man wanted to go with Jesus. In the man's mind, that's what he thought was the best way to serve God. Jesus had him do his will instead. It's so easy to get caught up in the hustle and bustle of every day. We can easily get distracted from serving the Lord. We must constantly remind ourselves that he is good and he loves us literally to death, and doing his will and loving him back in the same way is how we should all give him praise. He knows our future and our past. All we know is where we came from. We need to trust him to take us by the hand and lead us to where he wants us to go. We may not see it right away, but looking back at times in our lives, I'm sure all of us can see when God was working in them. If he was working in our lives then, wouldn't you think that he would be working in our lives now? I can honestly say that serving God over serving myself is much more rewarding. He has been working for us all our lives, even before we existed. Shouldn't we too perform tasks for him and with him daily to express our devotion to him? You deserve to be happy, and true happiness is found in serving Jesus. Don't think you must become holy to come to him. Jesus wants you to express your need for him. It is with him, and only with him, that we can become holy. Humble yourself, sinful and sorrowful, and come to Jesus just the way that you are.

Recap: Your sin has ruptured your relationship with God. You are not ready for your mission in this state.

Step 2: Write an apology letter to Jesus and a goodbye letter to your sins. Then humble yourself before Jesus at the tabernacle, the way that you are, and read your letters to him. Even though your sins may be scarlet, Jesus is always ready to welcome an honest and repentant heart back to him. Invite him in and be willing to let him change you, to reconnect you to his mystical body and prepare you for your mission.

This powerful prayer helped me come to Jesus when I was the worst of all sinners. I hope it helps you too.

Padre Rookies Miracle prayer:

Lord Jesus, I come before you just as I am. I am sorry for my sins; please forgive me. In your name, I forgive all others for what they have done against me. I renounce Satan, the evil spirits, and all their works. I welcome you into my life, Lord. Come change me, heal me, strengthen me in body, soul, and spirit. Come, Lord Jesus, cover me with your precious blood. Fill me with your Holy Spirit. I give you my entire self, Lord. I love you, Jesus; I praise you, Jesus. I shall follow you every day of my life.

This next prayer is in my words. (Both prayers should be said together.)

I implore you Blessed Mother, my mother, Queen of the Angels, mother of my heart, forever Virgin Mary to pray for me to the Lord Our God for special graces and strengths to help me amend my life and put me in perfect union with you. With the prayers of all the angels and saints in the kingdom of heaven, please come to my aid and assist me in the prolific works of serving God.

In your name, Jesus, this I pray, amen.

Jesus, I'm Sorry

Goodbye Sin

Into the Light We Go

NOW THAT WE have come to Jesus and have asked him to enter our hearts, he will now shine his light on all your imperfections, making you aware of what is displeasing to him and what is bad for you. Since the dawn of creation, we have relied on God to tell us what is right or wrong. Then Eve, when tempted by the devil, decided to be her own judge of right and wrong, convincing Adam to do likewise. Like Eve, you have been the judge of deciding what is right or wrong for yourself. It's time to let God be the judge of right and wrong in your life again. Let God shine his light into your heart and ask him to show all your offenses toward him and your neighbor.

If you are unsure of what actions may constitute an offense toward God, you can go to your local parish and ask to speak with a priest. Ask the priest for a confession pamphlet. Most of these pamphlets will cover a wide variety of offenses toward God, helping you understand the totality of your sins against him. You will begin to experience an internal struggle of emotions and sorrow for sin. Feeling this way means that you are sorry for what you have done, but most of all, you are sorry for hurting Jesus. This battle comes from the darkness that dwells inside of you, in sin. Remember, God did not create Adam and Eve with sin. They were made perfect in the glory of God. They brought sin into the world by their actions, just as you have allowed sin to enter your life by your actions. Don't feel too bad. This fallen nature is partially inherited from them. This darkness that is within you fears the light. That light is Jesus (John 8:12 RSV Catholic Edition). With Jesus with us, we have nothing to fear. Satan should fear you! You are a person dedicated and committed to getting in a right relationship with God, and you will fight to protect it. The dark side of you will do anything it can to stop you from continuing this path toward righteousness, holiness, and Jesus. Getting married is a step toward Jesus. Getting baptized is a step toward Jesus. Going to the sacrament of reconciliation is a step toward Jesus. Your first communion and confirmation are a step toward Jesus. All these acts put you in a right relationship with God. Prepare to fight the good fight!

Once you have an understanding that the way you have been speaking, acting, or teaching others, contrary to God's law, has been hurting the one who created you, you will begin to feel great guilt and shame for the wrongs that you have committed against him. If you continue to commit such acts, these emotions will become overwhelming. This is Jesus bringing us to repentance (Luke 5:32 RSV Catholic Edition). Jesus weighs us down with this emotion to cause us to change. As we draw closer to the Lord, he will shine his light on our souls, exposing the truth about us and causing us to have our own self-conviction. He will show us the sinful blemishes that have stained our souls so we may remove them with his help and the help of his church that is our community.

When Jesus raised Lazarus, whom he loved, from the dead, Lazarus came out of the tomb wrapped in grave clothes (John 11:43–44 RSV Catholic Edition). Jesus said to the others of the community that were watching, "Unbind him and let him go." In this story, the grave clothes that Lazarus was wrapped in represent our sins. Sin ties us up and leads us to the grave. Jesus commanded the community to help remove Lazarus's sin (the grave clothes) and let him go free. Jesus is telling us that we should seek not only his help but also the help of our community of believers, that is, his holy church, to help unbind us from our sin that leads us to death. Through reconciliation and prayer, people can remove these blemishes so they may return to the state of grace that Jesus never wanted them to fall away from in the first place.

The sacrament of reconciliation is an amazing way of utilizing the church and your community of priests to help unbind you of those grave clothes that have you all wrapped up in your sin. Many of the old-style Catholic churches have the confession booths with two sides to them with a partition in between. The side with the priest has a light on that shines through a screen into the side you are in, which is in darkness. This represents the priest being on the side with God, who possesses the light. When we are living in sin, we are living in darkness. This reminds us to come back to the light after we confess our sins. We open the door to the confessional, and we step out of sin and out of the darkness and back into the light where God dwells. We should take the expression of the light not just in the figurative sense, but literally also. The eighth of the fifteen promises of the rosary, which our Blessed Mother gave to Saint Dominic in an apparition, states, "Those who are faithful to recite the rosary shall have during their life and at their death the light of God and the plentitude of his graces; at the moment of death they shall participate in the merits of the saints in paradise." Our Queen, the Blessed Virgin Mary, is promising us the protection and the distribution of God's spiritual protection by means of his powerful spiritual light, both during our life and at the moment of our death. We should also look at the light of the day as a means of strength and assistance.

If you're learning something and you just can't seem to figure it out, try taking a break from your frustration and find a sunny place to sit in the light of the day. Spend a few moments with Jesus or our Blessed Mother in prayer and meditation. Afterward try going back to what you were trying to learn. I have found meaningful results with such a practice. John 11:6–10 RSV Catholic Edition states that Jesus arose and heard Lazarus was sick. He said to his disciples, "Let us go into Judea again," and the disciples stressed to him that the Jews sought to stone him. Are you going there again"?" they said. Jesus answered, "'Are there not twelve hours in the day? If anyone walks in the day, he does not stumble because he sees the light of this world. But if anyone walks at night, he stumbles because the light is not in him.'" Two days before they were in Judea, they were chased out of that city by the Jewish people. Jesus was teaching his disciples that it is better to go back in the light of the day because people get confused at night by the powers of darkness. Ephesians 6:12 RSV Catholic Edition states, "For we are not contending against flesh and blood, but against the principalities, against the powers, against the world rulers of this present darkness, against the spiritual hosts of wickedness in the heavenly places."

So, let us all in faith and in all aspects of our lives receive the light of the day, as well as the light of God, with great peace and humility. They are the gifts given to us from heaven that none of us deserve for the just man is a light in the darkness to the upright. Psalm 112:4–5 RSV Catholic Edition says, light rises in the darkness for the upright; the Lord is gracious, merciful and righteous. It is well with the man who deals generously and lends, who conducts his affairs with justice, "for just as Christ is the light of the world, so you are also Christ in the world. So, let your light shine bright to others." Apply what is written in Matthew 5:14–16: "You are the light of the world. A city set on a hill cannot be hid nor do men light a lamp and put it under a bushel, but on a stand, and it gives light to all in the house Let your light so shine before men, that they may see your good works and give glory to your Father who is in heaven..."

Shine your light on all our brothers and sisters so they can see Christ's light in you with acts of charity, compassion, long suffering, and love. In doing so we will be proving ourselves faithfully to our Lord Jesus and his mother, for it is in giving that we receive. By applying the teachings of Jesus, he will reveal to us our spiritual gifts. In the same way, he shines his light on all our imperfections and reveals our sins. Your virtues are up to you. Virtues are a strength that someone attains, and a grace from God is a gift that is given. By him doing this, it will give you a better understanding and direction of what your mission may be. Think of your soul in relation to remodeling the inside of your house. I would have to remove everything inside of it so I could make changes to it. In an equivalent way, the light of God reveals our sins so we can remove them to make space for us to attain new virtues. Allowing God's light to reveal our gifts, within these virtues, will remodel you, take out what is old and broken, fill you up with new graces, and lift your spirit to give you drive, purpose, and direction by means of his holy light.

Recap: Coming to Jesus with our sins is emotionally painful. We must trust him to help us expose our sins and not doubt his forgiveness and mercy to prepare us to do his will.

Step 3: Let God's light reveal your sins and take the initiative to remove them by the help of your community of priests and God's holy church. Write a poem to God about the way that you feel right now so you may read it at the end of this journey and show yourself how far you have come. This will help you cope with all the emotions that have been brought to the surface with God's holy light, exposing your sins so Jesus can remove them, leaving room for virtue so you may receive special graces from God that are to be illuminated in your heart.

Sign of the cross
Lord Jesus, it is said that your word is a lamp to my feet. May it guide me in the will of obeying your law to the love of my neighbor to bring me back to your heart, which is the source of light and the source of my joy , the object of my love and the center of my life.

In Jesus's name, amen.

Tell God How You Feel

Let Go of Your Sin and Reach for Virtue

NOW THAT WE see our sins and what they are, we see ourselves for what we have become. It's time for a spiritual spring cleaning, a renovation of the body. Ask yourself this question: When was the last time you went to reconciliation? One year, ten years, twenty years? If you answered yes to any of these, it's time that you take a shower. No, not a physical shower, a spiritual shower. In Luke 11:38–40 RSV Catholic Edition, Jesus sat down to eat with the Pharisees and did not wash his hands in accordance with the Law of Moses. When the Pharisees saw this, they were shocked. Then our Lord said to them, "Now you Pharisees cleanse the outside of the cup and of the dish. But inside you are full of extortion and wickedness. You fools! Did not he who made the outside make the inside also?" Jesus is telling us here that even if we consider ourselves good Christians because we go to church and read the Bible, it means nothing if we only clean the outside of our cups and visually appear holy. We must trust in God and have faith in his church and its sacraments that we may attain spiritual cleanliness by means of reconciliation and prayer. It's time to experience God's mercy and forgiveness in this sacrament.

This may be a little bit difficult to deal with emotionally, depending on the type of life you have led. You may feel embarrassed or think that the priest may judge you in some way. I promise you that there's nothing you can tell your priest that he hasn't heard before. I recommend if you haven't been in a while that you make an examination of conscience. You can do this by using pen and paper and one of those pamphlets on reconciliation that I mentioned earlier. Making a good examination of conscience is a good sign to Jesus that you are truly sorry for all that you have done against him and would like to be as thorough as possible in confessing your sins. If you don't want to take a paper-and-pen examination, you can ask the priest in the confessional to help you search your heart. He will ask you questions pertaining to breaking God's laws in any way and will help you recall any past acts and offenses. You may find that you have been committing mortal sins and may have not even known it, thus rupturing your relationship with God. Once you finish confessing your offenses, the priest will absolve you of your sins, reconnecting you in the great mystical body of Christ (1 Corinthians 12:27 RSV Catholic Edition). Sit in front of the tabernacle in the peace and quiet of the church and in God's great grace and mercy. Every time you go to reconciliation, you not only receive special graces from God as well as practicing the virtue of humility but also experience the spiritual effects of this sacrament, which are as follows:

1. Reconciliation with God by which the penitent recovers grace
2. Reconciliation with the church
3. Remission by the eternal punishment incurred by mortal sins

4. Remission, at least in part, of temporal punishment resulting from sin
5. Peace and serenity of conscience, and spiritual consolation
6. An increase of spiritual strength for the Christian battle.

(*Catechism of the Catholic Church*, second edition, p.374.)

On top of all of that, the graces (gifts) you receive from God are meant to assist you in accomplishing your purpose. It is different for everybody different gifts for different purposes as you can see from spiritual effect number four. It says, "Remission, at least in part, of temporal punishment resulting from sin." What this means is that the sin you committed is forgiven by God, but it has caused injustice to the fabric of our world. To be entirely forgiven of this sin, you must physically make right the wrong that you have committed. For example, if you stole money or goods from someone, you must give back what you have taken or more. We get this from the story of Zacchaeus (Luke 19:8 RSV Catholic Edition). When Jesus entered Jericho, there was a man named Zacchaeus, a tax collector, who wanted to see him. So, he climbed a tree to see over the crowd, for he was a short man. Jesus told him to come down, for the Lord was to stay at his house that night. Zacchaeus said, "Behold Lord, the half of my goods I give to the poor; and if I have defrauded any one of anything I restore it fourfold." (Tax collectors were notorious for overcharging households for tax so they could keep the portion that they overcharged.) Jesus then said to him, "Today salvation has come to this house since he also is a son of Abraham, for the Son of Man came to seek and save the lost." Jesus called Zacchaeus a son of Abraham because tax collectors were considered sinners and the Jewish people considered themselves not to be sinners. This means that Jesus was expressing that sinners can attain salvation as well.

So here we have a man who made up for his wrong before meeting Jesus to prevent chastisement, and he told the Lord that he had already paid back what he had wrongfully taken. We too must pay back what we have wrongfully taken before the day comes when our soul is required of us and we stand before Jesus in judgment, so we can say, "I am sorry for what I have done, Lord, and I have given back what I have taken. Please have mercy on me."

The other situation in which we see Jesus giving someone a chance to right a wrong is with Saint Peter. Peter denied the Lord three times before the rooster crowed. After Jesus was resurrected from the dead, he came to Peter and saw him fishing again. They sat by the fire to eat breakfast, and Jesus asked him three times, "Do you love me?" (John 21:15–17 RSV Catholic Edition). All three times Peter said yes to counteract the three times he had denied our Lord.

So, our journey is not over when we leave the confessional booth. We must take it one step further in our pursuit of righteousness and on our road to repentance. Some may ask, "Why go to a priest to confess my sins? Why can't I just confess my sins to God?" The priest has taken a vow to serve God as a vessel for the spirit of God to work through. True, the spirit of God works through us all, but the spirit of God works in a distinct way through the priest for all of us who seek the help of God. When Jesus was resurrected from the dead, he led his disciples to Bethany. He placed his hands on each of them and breathed on them, passing down to them his power to forgive sins, heal the sick, cast out demons, and raise the dead (John 20:23 RSV Catholic Edition).

God has used priests since the days of Moses. When the old law had first been given to the Hebrews (Exodus 28:1 RSV Catholic Edition), Jesus continued this tradition in his ministry as well. Priests have been given their title by laying their lives down to serve God and us all their life. In doing this, they have the authority from God and his holy church to speak and heal on his behalf. Forgiving sins, healing the sick, exorcising demons, and bringing someone back to life are all forms of healing. Through our faith, we are made well.

Let's look at Matthew 9:20 RSV Catholic Edition and the woman who was subject to bleeding. She had spent all her money on physicians to be healed only to have her problem worsen. For twelve years, she was bleeding. When she heard that Jesus was in town and knew of his miracles, she said to herself, "If I only touch his garment, I shall be made well." So, she made her way through the crowd. Many were around Jesus, brushing up against him. But when the woman came and touched his cloak, Jesus turned, and seeing her he said," take heart, daughter; your faith has made you well?" (Luke 8:45 RSV Catholic Edition). As soon as the woman touched his cloak, she was made well. this woman touched Jesus in faith. She believed that if only she could touch his cloak, she would be healed, and because of her faith in him, she was. Jesus felt his power leave him. He turned to her, and the woman confessed all that she had done by touching him. Jesus said to her, "Daughter, your faith has healed you; go in peace and be healed from your affliction."

I want you to understand that Jesus didn't even know this woman was there until she touched him in faith and belief. Without any doubt or speculation, we too must also have faith and belief in Jesus. When we confess our sins to our priests, we must have faith in Jesus and his priests, who possess the authority of God and his church that our sins are forgiven. With this powerful virtue of undoubtable faith in Jesus, many miracles can happen in our lives, in some cases before Jesus even knows we're there. It is our faith in him that restores us. It is our belief that he can restore us that makes it come true, just like the woman who touched his cloak. Confession is not only needed to clean us from sin, but it is also a powerful weapon against the forces of evil. Our faith is based on our free will. When we choose to attend this sacrament, we choose to humble ourselves before God and give him permission to help us in our lives. When we choose not to go, we choose to close ourselves off to God's forgiveness and mercy. By not choosing God, we leave ourselves open to other types of demonic forces. Father Garry Thomas, of the Sacred Heart Church, Diocese of San Jose, California, is an exorcist for the Catholic church. He states that "confession is more powerful than an exorcism. By going to reconciliation, you are not only severing all demonic ties, but you are also receiving special graces from God. If people went to reconciliation more often, it would be difficult for these entities to manifest."

Besides demonic possession, there is also demonic oppression. This is where an intelligent evil spirit has affixed itself around you and is causing you to feel depressed or angry, often at inopportune moments, to ruin joy in the family household or to constantly separate you from your loved ones. You may feel like it's your mood or your emotions. But these entities can manipulate your emotions and moods. They are parasites; they feed off your sorrow and the sorrow you cause others. Many of the people whom Father Thomas has helped have carriers and families. Most are not aware that something like this is even possible. For whatever reason, by not going to reconciliation you are providing a perfect home for a dark entity to live in or around you. Remember, these entities have been around for a very long time and are very good at what they do, especially at not revealing themselves too much so you notice that they are there. We cannot expect to compete with such a being. That's why we need God's help and protection. By going to reconciliation, you will be taking a spiritual shower, cleaning yourself of your sins. In the process of doing this, you may rid yourself of a dark entity that you never even knew was there.

Remember, God is love, peace, and joy. By reconnecting yourself to God, you will feel these emotions all the time. Whether you're rich or poor, brokenhearted, or suffering from an illness, by staying connected to the Lord you will always be joyful, you will always be at peace, and you will always feel loved. Look at the lives of the saints. Many of them left their families, were thrown in prison, or were beaten and ridiculed by people they knew for their love for Jesus. They gave away all their possessions and were poor and hungry, but they still were content and displayed happiness and peace. The more that they gave, the more they received because they were integrated into the great mystical body of Christ. They were connected to the source of pure joy, of pure peace, and to the divine love that is not of this world.

Recap: Reconciliation is a powerful tool, left for us from Jesus, and passed down to his disciples and from his disciples to the priests that we have today. By reconciling with God, you will be given special grace to help you with your mission as well as strength to help you overcome vice to aid you in the Christian battle. God is the source of pure and everlasting love, peace, and joy. Evil entities are out to destroy these emotions from your life and to destroy you. Choose to let Christ's might fight for you in this powerful sacrament.

Step 4: Make an examination of conscience, attend reconciliation regularly (at least once a month), and be absolved of your sins and of any demonic ties. Leave the confessional and step into the grace of God. Now go right your wrongs to amend the corporeal injustice that you brought into the world. Then bask in the contentment of being reconnected to the great mystical body of Christ and the great drive to pursue your purpose. Once you have been given strength and grace through reconciliation, you must counteract your sins with lively virtues. I have provided you with a list of the seven deadly sins and the seven lively virtues that counteract those sins. Notice which sins are predominant in your life, let go of them, and strive for the virtues that counteract your sin, so you may stay in a state of grace with God. So that he may eagerly give you the mission that you have strived so diligently to prepare for.

Sign of the cross
O Lord, help me to search my heart for all my imperfections that are displeasing to you. May your divine light illuminate them to help me confess them, so I may better love you and serve you, all the days of my life.

In Jesus's name, amen.

Examination of Conscience

Go to your local parish and ask for a guide to confession pamphlet

This will help you write down all your sins that you have committed against God that you may not have even known you have made against him.

Then take that list to our beloved priests to confess your sins

The Seven Deadly Sins

1. Lust (an excessive sexual desire)
2. Gluttony (habitual greed or excess in eating)
3. Greed (an insatiable longing for wealth)
4. Sloth (reluctance to work or try/idleness)
5. Wrath (outbursts of anger)
6. Envy (a resentful longing for what someone else has)
7. Pride (a deep pleasure or satisfaction derived from one's own achievements/vanity)

The Seven Lively Virtues

1. Chastity (refraining from sexual intercourse)
2. Temperance (moderation or self-restraint, especially from eating or drinking)
3. Charity (voluntarily helping those in need, typically in the form of money)
4. Diligence (careful and persistent work or effort)
5. Forgiveness (pardoning someone or receiving pardon from someone, or mercy)
6. Kindness (being friendly, generous, and considerate)
7. Humility (a modest or low view of one's own importance, humbleness)

Build Your Relationship

I'M SURE BY now you are feeling much lighter, more at peace, less anxious, more joyful. That's because sin weighs us down. Once Jesus has unburdened us of sin in the sacrament of reconciliation, we should be careful not to put that heavy weight back on us. Jesus will help us avoid this. To stay strong, we must stay connected to our source of strength. Having a relationship with Jesus is just like having a relationship with anybody else, whether it be a friend, parent, sibling, or spouse. If you neglect these people or don't make the time for them, they won't feel loved or appreciated. They also won't be able to give you any advice about whatever you may be going through in your life. It's the same thing with Jesus. If you don't spend time with him, you won't have much of a relationship. If you spend a lot of time with him, you will have a great relationship with him. It's as simple as that.

Now that you are renewed in Christ, it's time to add a holy hour to your day. Take the time to read the Bible, pray the rosary, and just spend time with Jesus and our Blessed Mother. Add this to your new lifestyle, keeping your relationship with Jesus strong. Change is good when it's toward God. He changes us into new and better people. Saint Thomas Merton once said, "Living is the constant adjustment of thought to life and life to thought. In such a way that we are always growing, always experiencing new things in the old and old things in the new, thus life is always new." Every step toward Jesus will change you, making you a new person. Praying the rosary, going to Mass, attending reconciliation, and reading the Bible or other forms of spiritual books will make your relationship with God stronger. Adding a daily holy hour to your new lifestyle will change the way you look at life and how you view the world around you. Your perspective about everything will change dramatically, especially if you pray the rosary.

At first, praying the rosary was a bit unorthodox for me because I converted from nondenominational Christianity, but the more I prayed with it, the more things started to change. I read my Bible every morning. Once I added praying the rosary to my holy hour, certain habits I had before went away. My temper became less volatile. I began writing a book to bear fruit for God. I felt less anxious, and my moods felt more level. All of this happened in just a brief time of praying the rosary consistently each day. Now I won't go a single day without praying the most holy rosary and meditating on its mysteries, especially after discovering the promises that our lady, the Virgin Mary, gave to Saint Dominic in an apparition in the year 1214 AD. to those who pray the rosary daily. The promises are as follows.

1. Whoever should faithfully serve me by recitation of the rosary shall receive signal graces.
2. I promise my special protection and the greatest graces to all those who recite the rosary.
3. The rosary shall be a powerful armor against hell; it will destroy vice, decrease sin, and defeat heresies.

4. It will cause virtue and good works to flourish. It will obtain for souls the abundant mercy of God. It will withdraw the hearts of men from the love of the world and its vanities, and will lift them to the desire of eternal things. Oh, that souls would sanctify themselves by this means.
5. The souls that recommend themselves to me by the recitation of the rosary shall not perish.
6. Those who shall recite the rosary devoutly, applying themselves to the consideration of its sacred mysteries, shall never be conquered by misfortune. God will not chastise them in his justice; they shall not perish by an unprovided death. If they be just, they shall remain in the grace of God and become worthy of eternal life.
7. Whoever should have a true devotion to the rosary shall not die without the sacraments of the church.
8. Those who are faithful to reciting the rosary shall have, during their life and at their death, the light of God and the plentitude of his graces. At the moment of death, they shall participate in the merits of the saints in paradise.
9. I shall deliver from purgatory those who have been devoted to the rosary.
10. The faithful children of the rosary shall merit a high degree of glory in heaven.
11. You shall obtain all you ask of me by recitation of the rosary.
12. All those who propagate the holy rosary shall be aided by me in their necessities.
13. I have obtained from my divine Son that advocates of the rosary shall have for intercessors the entire celestial court during their life and at the hour of death.

14. All who recite the rosary are my sons, and brothers of my only Son, Jesus Christ.
15. Devotion to my rosary is a great sign of predestination.

Having a devotion to the Mother of God by praying her rosary is a gift of prayer and a powerful weapon against evil that I wish I would have found long ago. When we have respect for our Lord's mother, he in turn has respect for us. He loves us, and by loving his most holy mother, Jesus gives us a special place in his heart. By devotion to him and her, we can ask for anything in accordance with his will. Everything that the saints accomplished was in accordance with God's will. Look to them as role models. Their actions emulate love for Jesus and his mother as well as righteousness and good works. You may ask yourself, "How can I do what the saints did, or the apostles for that matter? How can I leave a mark on this world that points souls to Jesus?" You may think you're not intelligent or diligent in your work. I know I did, but these are the people God loves to ask to do his greatest works. God does not choose the qualified for the work he needs done; rather he chooses the unqualified and then qualifies them to do the work. You see, most of the saints and the apostles were not intelligent people, but they all had one thing in common. They all had a relationship with Jesus through Mary. None of them had the capability or knowledge or skill to do what our Lord asked of them, just like you and me. God knows this. That's why whatever you are lacking, God will make up for in grace, thus giving you all the spiritual gifts, knowledge, and capabilities to be able to bear fruit, love thy neighbor, and complete your mission. God chooses ordinary people so that, with him, we become extraordinary people.

Let's look at the book of Acts 2:14–26 RSV Catholic Edition. After Pentecost, all the disciples and Mary were filled with the Holy Spirit. All of them could now speak languages that they had never known before. Saint Peter spoke with great boldness to the Pharisees, quoting the prophets from the Torah in accordance with the miracles Jesus had performed and testifying that Jesus was the messiah. The Pharisees were amazed and perplexed. They all knew Peter and the other eleven disciples. They knew he was just a fisherman. But by the gift of the Holy Spirit and by God's grace, they were all given the knowledge needed to accomplish their purpose. Just like the perplexed Pharisees, your friends and family may be perplexed by your newfound gifts because Jesus has changed you. He has chosen the foolish to shame the wise, the weak to shame the strong (1 Corinthians 1:27 RSV Catholic Edition). That is why we must pray to him and serve him by doing his will through the intercession of the most holy and blessed Virgin Mary, his mother and the mother of all believers.

There is nothing that we cannot ask of him that is in accordance with his will. There is nothing that we cannot accomplish with the power of All-Mighty God on our side. If it is not him whom you serve, ask yourself who or what do you serve? Do you get out of bed every morning to make money or to spend time with God first? Do you put your faith in a woman or a man? Why not put your faith in the one who gave you that person? Is your daily place of worship the gym or some other form of extracurricular activity, instead of making time to spend with the one who gave you this busy life in the first place? I'm not saying you should stop living a full life. I'm saying make Jesus the center of it. Make him your priority in your actions, in your speech, in your thoughts, in your everyday and let everything else in your life flow from that point. Jesus said, "He who believes in me, as the scripture has said, out of his heart shall flow rivers of living water." (John 7:38 RSV Catholic Edittion). Therefore, let everything in your life flow from your love for God, and let rivers of living water flow through you to your friends and family and those you love who are with you always. Pray, read, and listen; meditate on the life of Jesus and his bitter passion and your gratitude to him for creating you and dying for you to atone for your sins, so you can show your appreciation to your dearest friend. I'm sure many of us can say we have close friends, perhaps friends we have known all our lives. I'm sure most of us don't have any friends who have died for us. So, make the time for the only one who did. Set aside one hour every day for the one friend who saved you.

Recap: Jesus loves spending time with you. The more time you spend with him, the more hidden things he will reveal to you. If you feel he has asked you to do something that you don't think you can do, then you're on the right track. Don't worry; he will qualify you for the task.

Step 5: Incorporate a holy hour in your day. Read the Bible and books of the saints, pray the rosary daily, and sit in the quietness of prayer and listen for the voice of Jesus. Make a list of family and friends who have passed away and a list of people you know who may need prayers especially those who don't believe; they need your prayers most of all. Use this list daily to remind you to pray for them. You will find that your list will grow as time goes on. This list is an effective way to keep track of all the souls that need your prayers every day.

(Recommendation: pray your rosary daily and your entire life will change.)

Sign of the cross
O righteous and forgiving Father, jealous for my affection and longing for my time, please help me find the time each day to spend with you, the center of my life. It is you I serve, it is you I trust, and it is you I love. May your grace and peace flow through me to all those I know and care for. May the love of God be reflected in my actions and in my words.

In Jesus's name, amen.

By the intercession of the Blessed Virgin Mary and all the angels and saints, I pray for these souls:

Living	Passed on

Words Are Powerful

I'M SURE IF you have been following all the steps, you are feeling better than you ever have in your life. The closer you are to Jesus, the more immersed you are in his peace, love, and joy. It's truly amazing! Staying dedicated to your time spent with him every day continuously increases this sense of well-being.

In this next step, I want you to focus on the words you use every day, not only in your prayers but with others as well. Begin speaking to others the way that you speak to God in prayer. Words are powerful. Now that you are becoming more pious, you are drawing nearer to righteousness and a better, more fulfilling life. James 5:16 RSV Catholic Edition says, "Therefore confess your sins to one another and pray for one another, that you may be healed. The prayer of a righteous person is powerful and effective." In knowing this truth, it is also good to rest in the fact that right now, in this stage of your journey, Jesus will hear you more than ever. I had many of my prayers answered by God at this point in my journey. If there was ever a time to ask him for something, it would be now.

Matthew 7:11 RSV Catholic Edition states, "If you, then, who are evil, know how to give good gifts to your children, how much more will your Father who is in heaven give good things to those who ask him!" This verse is saying that, even though we are sinners and even when we are in a deep state of sin, we still give our children what they ask of us. It's a different story when our children are disobeying us. They will ask, and we will tell them, "No, you haven't been good" or "you haven't finished your homework" or "you haven't cleaned up your room, so you can't play video games." Or something along those lines. My point is this: we are more likely to give our children what they want when they have been good rather than when they have been bad. But, let's face it, many of us give in and give them what they want even when they have disobeyed us. God answers our prayers in the same way. Even when we have been bad, he still gives in, but it is better to ask him in a state of grace and love for him. Many of the saints had miraculous prayers answered when they were walking with God. Now that we are playing by his rules, he delights in giving us what we ask for. Not all prayers may be answered. Some of the things that you may ask Jesus for might be bad for you, even though you don't see anything wrong with them. God is the just judge, and we are no longer judging what is right or wrong in our lives. We are letting him be the judge so he can prepare us and protect us for what is coming in our future.

We must come to him in prayer for good counsel, asking him to bless us in all aspects of our lives, and thanking him for all the blessings he has poured upon us. It is good to pray and say, "Lord, I ask you for help in the morning and thank you for the help I have received in the evening, for you are great and just, O Lord." Every day we should say please and thank-you. Don't forget to thank God for those bad days also. Just remember, no matter how bad a day you might have had, it's nothing compared to the way Jesus suffered for you or how the saints were persecuted for their love of Jesus. When comparing your difficult day to theirs, it's no longer as bad as we thought in this state of grace and appreciation. We then thank Jesus for that so-called bad day. As stressful as it was, you still felt the sun on your face and saw the clouds in the sky and flowers blooming all around you.

Let us not take the simple things in this life for granted. Something as simple as being conscious of what words we say, or the way that we speak to one another, should be guarded carefully. Our words should be said in love. Dr. Masaru Emoto is a scientist who studies the effects of words and music in water. His research mainly concerns the thoughts and vibrations that affect the molecular structure of water. Dr. Emoto places samples of water in front of groups of people and has them say loving words or words of gratitude to the sample. Then Dr. Emoto freezes the water, and the ice crystals that form create incredible, beautiful designs and patterns. Different words create different patterns. He also does the same experiment using negative words of hate and ingratitude. The designs left after freezing these samples are not designs at all. The patterns left are abstract, distorted, and completely in disarray. He also uses polluted water and has it blessed with prayer. The water is no longer polluted after this, and those beautiful designs begin to appear again. This research is truly remarkable because the human body is made up of 65 percent water. So here we have scientific evidence supporting that idea that words can alter our physical state of being.

Auxiliary Bishop Robert Barron of the diocese of Los Angeles gave a commentary on the power of words from his online ministry, Word on Fire. He discussed how words not only change our mental well-being but they also can change our reality. He explains, "All of us can think back to when we were children or young adults and someone, whether it be a teacher or coach or parent, criticized us in a negative way, and we carried these words around with us all our lives. Now, whenever we attempt to accomplish something new or challenging, we may tell ourselves that we can't, or it's too difficult, because of these negative words that were said to us so long ago. In the same way that we carry those words around with us forever, we also carry around those words that a mentor had said to us that lifted us up and gave us encouragement. These positive words of encouragement are what help drive us to accomplish one challenging task after another. Throughout our lives, we always resort back to those words of encouragement that were said to us to provide us with the proper motivation that we need to accomplish our goal. So, in this example, we can see that words can change someone's emotional state of being, either to hinder them to accomplish a goal or to encourage them to succeed at it."

Bishop Barron goes on to speak about how words can alter our physical reality. "For example, if I tell you you're under arrest, you may laugh because I'm not a police officer, but if a police officer tells you are under arrest, you most definitely are under arrest. Or if an umpire in a baseball game tells you you're out, you most definitely are out. These people, carrying these types of titles in our society, have the authority to change our reality. You were under arrest because a police officer has the authority to arrest you. You were out in the baseball game because the umpire has the authority to say you're out."

"Now let's look at the words that God speaks. When God said, 'Let there be light,' light came forth (Genesis 1:3 RSV Catholic Edition) because God's authority is over all things and his words alter the reality of all things. "In the beginning was the Word, and the word was with God, and the word was God" (John 1:1 RSV Catholic Edition). 'And the word became flesh and dwelt among us, full of grace and truth; we have beheld his glory, glory as of the only begotten son from the Father' (John 1:14 RSV Catholic Edition). So, Jesus, being the word, made flesh that was in the beginning with God, and had the authority of God, because he is God-made flesh. When Jesus ate with his disciples at the last Passover meal, he took one piece of bread, broke it, gave everyone a piece, and said, 'This is my body which is given for you. Do this in remembrance of me.' Then he gave thanks and offered the wine to them, saying, 'This cup which is poured out for you is the new covenant in my blood.' (Luke 22:19–20 RSV Catholic Edition). Because Jesus is God-made flesh, his words have the authority to change the physical reality of the world around us. This means that when Jesus says that the bread is his body, it changes into his physical body. When he says the wine is his blood, it physically changes to his blood. Jesus said to them, 'truly, truly, I say to you, unless you eat the flesh of the son of man and drink his blood, you have no life in you; he who eats my flesh and drinks my blood has eternal life, and I will raise him up on the last day. For my flesh is food indeed, and my blood is drink indeed. He who eats my flesh and drinks my blood abides in me, and I in him. As the living Father has sent me, and I live because of the Father, so he who eats me will live because of me. This is the bread that came down from heaven, not such as the fathers ate and died; he who eats this bread will live forever' (John 6:53 RSV Catholic Edition). So, when our priests, who have the power from Jesus passed down to his disciples and given to them through the ages, consecrate the host during the mass, the spirit of God enters the host and physically changes the bread and the wine into the body and the blood of our Lord, Jesus Christ. Because of our priests' title, their words of authority to change the physical reality of the bread and wine to the actual body and blood of our Lord Jesus Christ come true by the spirit of God passed down from Jesus to the disciples and through the hands of our priests, no other church can make this claim. A husband's words have authority over his wife, and as a wife's words have authority over her husband (Ephesians 5:22–33 RSV Catholic Edition).

I hope you now realize the powerful meaning and effect words have on our physical and emotional state of being. We should do our very best to speak to one another with the grace, strength, honor, and dignity that God gave to all of us, for we were all made in his image, (Genesis 1:27 RSV Catholic Edition) and therefore, we should use only appropriate words when speaking to all people. Imagine if no one cursed, no one yelled at, or no one insulted another person. What a peaceful world this would be. 1 Peter 4:11 RSV Catholic Edition says, "Whoever speaks, as one who utters oracles of God; who-ever renders service, as one who renders it by the strength which God supplies; in order that in everything God may be glorified through Jesus Christ. To him be long glory and dominion forever and ever. Amen."." So, if we all speak the very words of God, the words that we say should be pure, as God is pure. Ephesians 4:29 RSV Catholic Edition states, "Let no evil talk come out of your mouths, but only such as is good for edifying, as fits the occasion, that it may impart grace to those who hear."." I say to you, speak to each other with words of kindness and compassion, my brothers and sisters, with the love and respect that our Father in heaven intended them to be used for.

Recap: Words are more powerful than you think. The words we use in our daily lives can build others up or break them down. A person's title will give him or her authority over certain aspects of our physical environment. Changing the way, you speak to all people will reflect Jesus in you and will flood your life with love.

Step 6: Change the way you speak to others. To help you with this, make a swear jar. Every time you say a curse word, put some money into it. Then give that money to the poor during Lent. Do this until you stop cursing. Once that happens, continue giving to the poor in thanks for Jesus helping you to stop cursing. All words that are negative in meaning should be removed from your speech. All words of encouragement should be added. Latin is a pure language, specifically because of the power of words. To control our speech is to remember how to blush. Let us encourage our neighbors instead of putting them down.

Sign of the cross
Almighty and merciful Father, I have not used your powerful gift of words in the manner that you had intended me to do so. Please have mercy on me and impart to me the ability and strength to change the way I speak to others, to more properly be a representative of your divine grace and love of all people.

In Jesus's name, amen.

Please cut out this little sign to tape on your swear jar to remind you what the money is for.

For the poor

and my repentance

Guide Me, Most Holy Spirit

NOW THAT YOU have a better understanding of the power of words, I want you to use those powerful words in prayer to ask the Holy Spirit to help guide you through your life. Remember, by your words you will be justified, and by your words you will be condemned (Matthew 12:37 RSV Catholic Edition). We have free will, so we must ask for help from God in order for him to help us. The Holy Spirit is the shared love between God, the Father, and Jesus (Bishop Robert Barron, Word on Fire ministry). When we accept Jesus, we too take part in this shared love. Just before Jesus ascended to heaven, he told his disciples, "Nevertheless I tell you the truth. It is expediant that for you that I go away, for If I go not away, the comforter will not come unto you" (John 16:7 RSV Catholic Edition). This gracious act of allowing us to be connected to this shared love is a true expression of divine charity. In the same way that Jesus gave us the Holy Spirit, we should give unto our neighbors in acts of charity and kindness, allowing that divine love of the Father and the Son to flow through us to others.

Many of us, at some point in our lives, have asked God to show us that he is real. We may have asked him, "If you're real, make this happen or that happen." It does, and from that point on, we begin to believe and start searching for more instances to see God reveal himself to us. In the same way that God continuously proves himself to us, we should also prove ourselves to him with acts of charity toward our neighbor and acts of charity toward God by giving him our time every day to do his work. Loving thy neighbor is the perfect way to show your love for God, as well as for your fellow man. Bishop Robert Barren commented on the Holy Spirit from his Word on Fire online ministry. He stated that if you are being led by the Holy Spirit, you are taking the path that is most charitable. In other words, when we make a choice, we should choose the one that expects more from us, whether it be time or money. Perhaps it would be more work than less work. The point is we are choosing to love each other simply for the greater good of the other person—to do something and to expect nothing in return. Now you are being led by the Holy Spirit. Now you are being led by love. So how can we indicate that the Holy Spirit is flourishing within us? In Galations 5:17 RSV Catholic Edition, Saint Paul speaks of the fruits of the Holy Spirit and what is not of the Holy Spirit. These are the works of the flesh. "For the desires of the flesh are against the spirit, and the desires of the spirit are against the flesh; for these are opposed to each other, to prevent you from doing what you would. But if you are led by the spirit you are not under the law. Now the works of the flesh are plain: imorality, impurity, licentiousness, Idolatry, sorcery, enmity, strife, jealousy, anger, selfishness, dissention, party spirit, envy, drunkeness, carousing and the like I warn you, as I warned you before, that those who do such things shall not enherit the kingdom of God. But the fruit of the Spirit is love, joy, peace, patience, kindness, goodness, faithfulness, gentleness, self-control; against such there is no law." (Galatians 5:17-23 RSV Catyholic Edition).

Saint Paul has given us an effortless way of assessing our lives, by seeing what category we fall under, to better help us to stay in communion with God. When we think of love, we think of joy and those warm, fuzzy feelings, but love is much more complex and powerful than just a happy emotion. Love will send a mother into a burning building to save her child. Love will cause a single man to marry a single mother and make a lifelong commitment to be a father. Love will cause a man to dig through the rubble of a collapsed building after an earthquake to find his beloved pet. Love caused God to become man, to take our sins upon himself when we didn't care about him, to be sacrificed to save all who would believe in him. Love is brave, courageous, fearless, hopeful, and unwaveringly powerful.

Saint Maria Faustina Kowalska is a beloved saint who was visited many times by an apparition of Jesus. This is someone who knew the embodiment of true love well. This is what she wrote in her diary (Diary of Maria Faustina Kowalska Notebook 1, page 378) about love: "Pure love is capable of great deeds and is not broken by difficulty or adversity, as it remains strong in the midst of great difficulties. So, too, it preserves in the toilsome and drab life of each day. It knows that only one thing is needed to please God. To do even the smallest thing out of great love, love and always love. Pure love never errs. Its light is strangely plentiful. It is ingenious at doing what is more pleasing to God, and no one will equal it. It is happy when it can empty itself out and burn like a pure offering. The more it gives of itself, the happier it is, but also, no one can sense dangers from afar as can love. It knows how to unmask and knows with whom it has to deal."

Many of the saints who were ordinary people, like you and me, understood the power of love given to us by means of the Holy Spirit. Like them, we should trust in the Holy Spirit to lead us on the proper path to Jesus. This great overpowering, defending force of love can reveal to you your spiritual gifts and will lead you to the path that God has designed for you to walk. Remember, you're ordinary so God wants to tell a story through your life to show the world that when someone has faith in him, he or she is capable of absolutely anything. When we reach for the fruits of the Holy Spirit, the works of the flesh will begin to fall away. This takes discipline. Satan will come and tempt you at key moments to try to draw you back into sin. This is a good indication that the path you are on is not the path of the devil, and the path that you are walking now is toward God.

So, if the path that you were on before wasn't leading toward God, where did that path lead to? If God is light, what is the opposite of light? If God is joy, what is the opposite of joy? If God is life, what is the opposite of life? So, the path that you once were on was rebelling from God as Lucifer still does. He tells people to live the way that they wish, to not live by the rules of God's love but to be our own judge of right or wrong, just like he convinced Eve to do. When you begin to move in the right direction, on the proper path toward repentance, he will try everything to pull you back to your original life. Jesus died for humankind, not for the fallen angels. This means if we believe in him and repent, we can be forgiven and saved, but Lucifer cannot. God loves us so much, and for Lucifer to hurt God, he will take as many of us with him as he possibly can. So, we must fight him in moments of temptation with the power of prayer. He is attacking you spiritually so you must defend yourself spiritually. It's not easy, but it's simple. James 4:7 RSV Catholic Edition says, "Submit yourselves therefore to God. Resist the devil, and he will flee from you." So, ask the Holy Spirit to help you overcome such desires. You can try this prayer; it was given to me by one of our priests at my parish:

"In the name of Jesus Christ and by the power of the Holy Spirit, I command you, unclean spirit, to leave my home." I use that one from time to time, but my true protection comes from the power of Mary's rosary.

If you just can't stay on track with the steps in this book, please pray your rosary daily. Remember, when tempted, God will always show you a way out (1 Corintians 10:13 RSV Catholic Edition). The devil is most likely giving you extra attention because you have something great to offer God that would hinder the devil and his schemes, especially if it helps others. God pays close attention to you when you constantly help others. Bishop Robert Barren describes the three elements that are related to the Holy Spirit: water, fire, and wind. He explains how these three elements can be harmless enough, but in nature they cannot be controlled. He talks about how a hurricane cannot be stopped. Or how a brush fire can get out of control very quickly. All firefighters can do is wait for it to burn itself out. Or how a tornado can tear through a town leaving devastation in its wake. This is the type of power the Holy Spirit possesses. The Holy Spirit is God. When we call upon this third entity of the trinity, we are calling upon that divine, charitable love that would rush into a burning house to save us. That same love would dig through the rubble of a collapsed building to find us. The Holy Spirit is our unstoppable defender whom we can call on at a moment's notice because the Holy Spirit never leaves us (John 14:15–31 RSV Catholic Edition). It is always there, waiting to receive our call for help, to reveal to us some special insight to our lives, to give us perspective on situations, and to lead us into acts of charity. The Holy Spirit guides us to the proper path that leads to Jesus and heaven, and reveals to us what spiritual gifts or tools we have been given to help accomplish our mission and attain eternal life.

Recap: The Holy Spirit is the shared love between God, the Father, and his only begotten Son, Jesus Christ. We too are connected to this unstoppable, overpowering, saving love of pure righteousness that is with us always (John 14:16 RSV Catholic Edition).

Step 7: Review the fruits of the Holy Spirit and the works of the flesh in Galatians 5:17. Give yourself an assessment by making a list of the works of the flesh and the gifts of the spirit. Write each in its own column so you can compare. Now circle all that pertain to you to see what category you fall under so you can begin to strive for the fruits of the spirit with acts of charity and love. Do not focus on what you want to stop doing; rather focus on what you want to make happen. You want to impress upon God that you love him and that you wish to pursue righteousness in faith and in all good works to attain the fruits of the Holy Spirit. Through helping others, you can become aware of your spiritual gifts.

Sign of the cross
O Holy Spirit, my helper, my comforter, my defender, spirit of truth. Please present me with opportunities to offer my love in acts of charity, kindness, gentleness, joy, and peace. May I be a vessel of your love to flow through and reach all those in my family, in my community, and around the world. Come, O most Holy Spirit, please be my guide in my life and defend me in my spiritual battles through the means of my prayers.

In Jesus's name, amen.

Works of the Flesh	Gifts of the Holy Spirit

Love All People

"LOVE THY NEIGHBOR" is, in my opinion, the greatest law that God could have ever given to us. If everyone followed this commandment, the world would be a better place. When Jesus was preaching about this commandment, a teacher of the Law of Moses stood up and asked Jesus, "Who is my neighbor?" He asked this question because in those days the Jewish people did not speak to or have any affiliation with anyone who wasn't Jewish. Jesus responded by telling the parable of the Good Samaritan (Luke 10:25–37 RSV Catholic edition). Jesus said, "A man was going down from Jerusalem to Jericho when he was attacked by robbers. They stripped him of his clothes, beat him, and went away, leaving him half dead. Now by chance,a priest (of the Jewish faith) happened to be going down the same road, and when he saw the man, he passed by on the other side. So, too, a Levite when he came to the place and saw him, also passed by and did not help him. But a Samaritan as he came where the man was, and when he saw him, he took pity on him. He went to him and bandaged his wounds, pouring on oil and wine. Then he put the man on his own donkey, brought him to an inn, and took care of him. The next day he took out two denarii (coins) and gave them to the innkeeper. 'Look after him,' he said, 'and when I return, I will reimburse you for any extra expenses you may have.'" Then Jesus said, "Which of these three was a neighbor to the man who fell into the hands of robbers?" The expert of the law replied, "The one who had mercy on him." Jesus then told him, "Go and do likewise."

You may think, how could the scribes and the Pharisees of that time be so lacking in compassion? The truth is we see this type of heartlessness every day. Think how often you see our homeless brothers and sisters on the street and see many people pass by without even a glance, or without giving alms or even saying hello. I'm sure some of us have done it ourselves. I tell you the truth, my brothers and sisters, find compassion in your heart for your fellow man. Besides writing, I also have a day job as a refrigeration technician. I was en route to my first call one morning when I noticed a young man, who appeared to be homeless, stumbling across the street. I passed him and looked in my rear-view mirror. I saw him sitting on the divider island in the middle of the street. I stopped to check on him and then saw that he was lying down on the center divider. Many people slowed down to look at him, but no one stopped to check on him. As I came closer, I noticed a small, plastic sun-faded Jesus nailed to the telephone pole on my way to check on the young man. I kissed my fingers and touched it as I crossed the street. Upon approaching the young man, I noticed his clothes were very dirty, he smelled quite bad, and his pants were ripped and hanging off of him. His breathing was becoming faint, and he was unresponsive. I called 911 and called across the street to two men to help me move him. As we did, I noticed that he had wet himself. I wanted to take him to the bus stop, but the two men who were helping me would not carry him any farther. We set him underneath that little sun-faded Jesus on the telephone pole. I tried pulling his pants up to give him some dignity, but they didn't move up very much. The paramedics arrived, cut off his shirt, and immediately began CPR. This young man clearly needed help long before the Holy Spirit and my guardian angel led me to help him. All I could do was stand there and pray for him. Hail Marys and Our Fathers were all I could think of in asking our Lord to have mercy on him. They performed CPR for forty-five minutes. As hard as they tried, that young man took his last breath and died on the sidewalk underneath that sun-faded plastic Jesus. Thinking back, I wish I would have baptized him or held his hand. He died with no family around him, no one he knew, all alone on a street corner, forgotten. He was our brother, and no one wanted to help him, just like the Pharisees and scribes of the time when Jesus was walking the earth, preaching his ministry. No one stopped his or her vehicle to get out to help him. They just looked at him as they drove by.

When you see the poor on the street, take the time to check on them, to give to them, to say hello. You never know if they may be dying and in need of love in their last moments here on earth. Mother Teresa believed in giving love to the ones who were cast out into the streets to die. When she found them sick and dying, she showed them love and compassion in their last moments. For someone to receive love, when no one has given them any for a very long time, changes the peace of someone's spirit even in death. Mother Teresa once said, "Being unwanted, unloved, uncared for, forgotten by everybody, I think that is a much greater hunger, a much greater poverty than the person who has nothing to eat." When we see our homeless brothers or sisters on the street, we should talk with them, shake their hand, and maybe even give them a hug. The best things in this life cannot be bought. I cannot tell you how appreciative most of them are when you spend some time talking with them and giving them some money. They are so grateful that you gave them the time of day. For that moment, they feel respected as all people should feel. We all possess the dignity of God because we are all made in his image (Genesis 1:27 RSV Catholic Edition/Mother Teresa). Respect is something that we all want from others. Many of the homeless I meet thank me for talking with them more than giving them money. Saint Maria Faustina Kawolska said in her diary, "If I cannot give them money, I give them kind words, and if I cannot give them kind words, I pray for them" (*Diary of Saint Faustina, Marian Press,1987)*.

Many of us search our whole lives for the perfect woman or man in the pursuit of love because love is a gift. We should give it freely as intended to those who have none. Most would rather be shown love, compassion, and respect than receive money. Still, it is our responsibility as good Christians of our community to give alms and to care for the forgotten. If we have it, we should give, and if we have a little, we should still give. We know this from the story of the widow who gave two mites. When Jesus was in the Jewish temple, he noticed that some rich people were giving to the treasury, and he saw also a certain poor widow putting in two mites. He said, "Truly I tell you, this poor widow has put more into the treasury than all the others. They all gave out of their wealth; but she, out of her poverty, put in everything she had, her whole living" (Mark 12:43–44 RSV Catholic Edition). Sometimes we may have our last five dollars in our pocket, but rather than keep it, we should give it away, for it is in giving that we receive. So, let us give out of our need, out of our livelihood. When we give away what little we have, we trust in God to take care of us. Matthew 6:26 RSV Catholic Edition says, "Look at the birds of the air; they neither sow nor reap nor gather into barns, and yet your heavenly Father feeds them. Are you not of more value than they?"

When we have complete trust in God, we find our reliance on him. In loving our neighbor and helping all people in the name of Jesus, we will be shown our purpose, given our mission, and walk the path God has designed for us that leads to him. Saint Ignatius once said, "Let us give and let us not count the cost." Wise words from this great saint, for God will give to you the way that you give to others. "Give and it will be given to you. good measure, pressed down, shaken together, running over, will be put into your lap. For the measure you give will be given back to you" (Luke 6:38 RSV Catholic Edition). So, let us have faith in good works and charity to show Jesus that we love him. James 2:22 RSV Catholic Edition says, "You see that his faith was active along with his works, and faith was completed by works". So, give alms, show compassion and kindness, and most of all, love thy neighbor.

Recap: Love your fellow man. It is in giving that we receive. In serving others, we serve Jesus. In the same measure that you gave it out, so it will be given out to you. Your mission will always be involved with serving others.

Step 8: Think of ways that you can give to the poor, whether it be food, money, clothing, or a conversation. When you give to the poor, let them have the greater part of what you possess, and you keep the lesser part. In doing this you will store up for yourselves treasures in heaven, where moth or rust does not destroy and where thieves do not break in and steal (Matthew 6:20). Each month purchase something for the poor and attach to it a verse that I have provided to remind them that God loves them. After you use up the verses that I provide, open your Bible and look up some verses on your own. If you seek, you will find (Matthew 7:07 RSV Catholic Edition). Let us show compassion for one another, especially to the ones who feel forgotten. Please show them that God still loves them and you do too.

Sign of the cross
Prayer of Saint Francis:

Lord, make me an instrument of thy peace

Where there is hatred, let me sow love

Where there is injury, pardon

Where there is doubt, faith

Where there is despair, hope

Where there is darkness, light

Where there is sadness, joy.

O Divine Master, grant that I may not so much seek to be consoled as to console

To be understood as to understand

To be loved as to love

For it is in giving that we receive

It is in pardoning that we are pardoned

And it is in dying that we are born into eternal life.

Hope

Cut out these verses and tape them to whatever items you wish to give to those in need. In doing so, you will not only be providing necessities for that person, but you will also be providing hope and contributing to the great body of Christ in spreading the word of God.

1 Samuel 2:8 RSV Catholic Edition
He raises the poor from the dust and lifts the needy from the ash heap; he sits them with princes and has them inherit a seat of honor. For the pillars of the earth are the Lord's; and on them he has set the world.

Isaiah 41:10 RSV Catholic Edition
fear not, for I am with you; do not be dismayed, for I am your God. I will strengthen you, I will help you; I will uphold you with my victorious right hand.

Joshua 1:9 RSV Catholic Edition
Have I not commanded you? Be strong and of good courage. be not frightened, neither be dismayed, for the Lord your God is with you wherever you go.

2 Corinthians 1:3–4 RSV Catholic Edition
Blessed be the God and Father of our Lord, Jesus Christ, the Father of mercies and God of all comforts, who comforts us in all our affliction, so that we can comfort those who are in any affliction, with the comfort with which we ourselves are comforted by God.

Remember Who Jesus Came For

YOU HAVE COME a long way. If you're anything like me, you have fallen down a couple of times. That's okay. That's why I want to take this time to reflect on who Jesus came to help. I want you to understand the love and forgiveness Jesus has for the ones who thought they could never be holy, the ones who just couldn't get things right. So, when you fall, you get back up. This is how saints are made. When they fall, they humble themselves before the Lord. They get back up and try again. I want you to notice, when you do fall, to look back at the vices, habits, and sins that you have already conquered. Every time I fell, it was a couple of times for the same sin; however, slowly but surely the harder I tried they drifted away. Please do not get discouraged and please don't give up. Look at the sins you have overcome and use that for encouragement toward which sins you are trying to overcome. God wants you to succeed; he wants all of us in heaven with him. It's up to us to choose to go there. He knows you, and he knows what you are trying to do. Through the intercession of the Blessed Virgin Mary and Blessed Saint Joseph, her spouse, and all of the angels and saints, Jesus will provide you with all the grace that you need to overcome all sin. He knows what you are trying to do takes practice and his mercy.

Saint Peter asked Jesus, "How many times should I forgive my brother? Seven times?" Jesus responded, "I do not say to you seven times but seventy times" (Matthew 18:21 RSV Catholic Edition). Jesus is always ready to forgive us so we can get back up and fight the good fight toward holiness—as long as we don't take his forgiveness for granted and we are legitimately trying to overcome sin. It's okay to feel like you are not a holy person. You are exactly who Jesus came to save. When the Pharisees saw Jesus talking with the prostitutes and the tax collectors, the Pharisees asked his disciples, "Why does he eat with tax collectors and sinners?" And when Jesus heard it, he, said to them, "those who are well have no need of a physician,but those who are sick; I came not to call the righteous, but sinners." (Mark 2:15-17 RSV Catholic Edition). When you feel defeated, like you can't do this, remember that Jesus came for the ones who couldn't do this—that, with him, they may succeed. Jesus said, "The thief comes only to steal and to kill and destroy; I have come that they may have life, and that they may have it more abundantly" (John 10:10 RSV Catholic Edition).

Let's review the story of the woman at the well (John 4:7–30 RSV Catholic Edition). Jesus stopped at the well in the heat of the day (about noon). A woman was there drawing water. The time of day is very important here because most of the town went to draw water early in the morning; it was too hot in the middle of the day. She was there, at that time, because if she went in the morning, she would be ridiculed, judged, and gossiped about by her neighbors for living with a man she was not married to. I would like to note here that if you find yourself gossiping from time to time about others, please remember that many child and young adult suicides have been linked to gossiping and rumors. If you are gossiping, please understand that you are participating in something nefarious. Ask yourself, if I were to talk this way about this person in front of him or her, how would it make this person feel? If it would hurt the individual, you shouldn't be talking about it. Where there are secrets and division, there is sin.

Now back to the woman at the well. While she was drawing water, Jesus asked her for a drink. She was shocked that he asked her because Jewish people would not share utensils with those who were not Jewish. Nor would they interact with anyone who was not Jewish. She said, "How is it that you, a Jew, ask a drink of me, a woman of Samaria?" Jesus answered her, "If you knew the gift of God and who it is that is saying to you give me a drink, you would have asked him, and he would have given you living water." Then the woman said to him, "Sir, you have nothing to draw with, and the well is deep; where do you get that living water? Are you greater than our father Jacob, who gave us the well and drank from it himself, and his sons, and his cattle? Jesus said to her, "Everyone who drinks of this water will thirst again, but whoever drinks of the water that I shall give him will become in him a spring of water welling up to eternal life." The woman said to him, "Sir, give me this water, that I may not thirst, nor come here to draw." Jesus said to her, "Go call your husband and come here." She replied, "I have no husband." Jesus said to her, "You are right in saying, I have no husband. For you have had five husbands, and he who you now have is not your husband; this you said truly." The woman said, "Sir, I perceive you are a prophet. Our fathers worshipped on this mountain, and you say that in Jerusalem is the place where men ought to worship."." "Woman," Jesus replied, "believe me, the hour is coming when neither on this mountain nor in Jerusalem will you worship the father.. You worship what you do not know. We worship what know, for salvation is from the Jews. But the hour is coming, and now is, when the true worshippers will worship the father in the spirit and truth for such the father seeks to worship him. God is spirit, and those who worship him must worship in the spirit and truth." The woman said to him, "I know the messiah is coming he who is called Christ, and when he comes he will tell us all things." Jesus said to her, "I who speak to you am he." At this point his disciples came and marveled that he talked with a Samaritan woman. Yet no one asked, "What do you wish?" or "Why are you talking with her?" The woman then left her water jar, went into the city, and said to the men, "Come see a man who told me all the things that I ever did. Could this be the Christ?" Then they left the city and came to him.

Jesus chose this ordinary Samaritan woman, who was the gossip of the town, to give all hope to us unholy people out there. She was not living a holy life as most of us had not before we came to know Jesus. Yet Jesus revealed some hidden truths to her, and she was amazed—so much so that she became the world's first evangelist. She ran into town and told many people the good news, that a man who says he is the messiah is here; come and see him. She wasn't a person who was good at living a righteous lifestyle, yet Jesus chose her to enlighten his disciples and us. Even though we are in sin and can't seem to live life the way God has designed, Jesus invites us to him to be healed, to be given some work to do for him. The woman at the well left her mark on history as the first Christian evangelist. Talk about going from ordinary to extraordinary! All she did was go to draw water, and Jesus called her. Jesus is calling you now. You are important to Jesus, and you play a valuable role in his plan. Don't let the devil's distractions and temptations keep you from contributing to God's people; don't give up. Jesus died for all of us while we were still sinners so that you and I can get back up and finish the excellent work that we were all born to do.

Recap: If you have stumbled, don't stay down. Get back up. Jesus came for all people, especially for those who can't seem to get things right. It takes your determination and his grace and mercy to keep you on this road that leads to heaven.

Step 9: Reflect on how far you have come. If you have fallen since you started this journey, get back up and pray your rosary daily; it is our weapon against evil. Jesus came to save and heal all people, especially people like you and me. Trust in his mercy, and believe through faith in him that he can and will do all that he can to keep you on this path. Don't be so hard on yourself. If you're trying to stand against temptation, don't! Avoid it instead. Don't put yourself in situations that will lead to sin. Remember, it's not a sin to be tempted. It's a sin to commit the act. Jesus will not turn you away if you humble yourself before him and keep fighting the good fight. If you need to return to confession, go and pick up where you left off. Then go to adoration and sit in the presence of God. It is a wonderful way to sort through your thoughts. Write down how you feel when you first arrive, as well as what you're thinking about and any emotions and thoughts that may come up during adoration. Once adoration has ended, write down how you feel and what thoughts you may have. You will feel much more at peace after sitting in the presence of Jesus. In three days, read what you have written and see if your perspective has changed.

Sign of the cross
Lord Jesus, I humble myself before you, sinful and sorrowful. I am striving to better myself and seeking to do your will. Please bestow on me the strength, dedication, and determination I need to remain in a state of grace with you all my life. I love you and will not take you for granted. May your merciful blood cover my sorrowful heart. This I pray by the intercession of the Blessed Virgin Mary and Blessed Saint Joseph, her spouse. Amen.

How do you feel?

What's on your mind?

How do you feel?

What's on your mind?

How do you feel?

What's on your mind?

Behold Your Mother

DECIDING NOT TO give up and to continue your path toward Christ is a daunting task. The enemy constantly fills your head with lies, trying to make you believe that you're not good enough. This eventually goes away and you begin to realize God's plan for you. Meditating on who Jesus came for helps me, and I hope it helps you also. Coming from a nondenominational Christian background, I had come to know Jesus well before I entered the doors of the Catholic church, but I still was not living a holy life. This is when I met the Mother of God, the Virgin Mary. I entirely attribute my conversion to the Catholic faith to Jesus through Mary.

To know our Blessed Mother is to know Jesus and his full redeeming mercy. Without Mary, we never would have had Jesus. God wasn't the only one who gave us his only Son. God the Father chose her to bring our salvation into this world. Mary and Joseph protected him when hiding from King Herod in Egypt. She cared for him as a good Jewish boy, taught him manners, and showed him love. She still does this for all of us who seek her assistance today.

Throughout history we see God renewing the old in the new, from the story of Abraham and Sarah (Genesis 18:11 RSV Catholic Edition) to Zachariah and Elizabeth (Luke 1:5–25RSV Catholic Edition). Both men were told that their wives, who were much older, were going to have children, and both women were past child-bearing years. Abraham was told by God, and Zachariah by an angel. Neither man believed what they were told. In fact, they both laughed when they heard it. Yet their wives bore sons. In another story, we see Moses going up to Mount Sinai to commune with God the Father. When Moses returned down the mountanin to address his people, his face was shinning with light (Exodus 34:29 RSV Catholic Edition) In the same way, when Jesus climbed to the top of Mount Tabor with Peter, James, and John, we see Jesus's face change and his clothes turn dazzling white. Here we see him communing with Moses, Elijah, and God the Father (Matthew 17 RSV Catholic Edition). The only difference between both stories on the mountain is that Jesus brought Peter, James, and john with him. Why? Because in the past, in the story of Moses on Mount Sinai, only Moses could stand on the mountain with God because he was chosen by God to be pure. When you're with Jesus, you can stand in God the Father's presence because he is entirely pure for us; because of Jesus, we become worthy. Again, we see the sacrificial lamb of the Passover being spotless with unbroken legs. The Hebrews were instructed to adorn the door posts with the blood of the lamb, and they did it by means of a hyssop (Exodus 12:21 RSV Catholic Edition). Then we see Jesus, the spotless lamb, being sacrificed for us (Romans 3:25 RSV Catholic Edition). Both the good thief and the bad had their legs broken on the cross, but Jesus's legs were not (John 19:32 RSV Catholic Edition). Instead they lanced his side, piercing his heart (John 19:34 RSV Catholic Edition). Just before he died, Jesus said, "I thirst," and the Roman guard gave Jesus some sour wine mixed with gall on the end of a hyssop (Matthew 27:34 RSV Catholic Edition). Again, we see our Lord and Savior being born through the womb of our Virgin Mother (Luke 2:1–20 RSV Catholic Edition), and after he died, they placed his body in a sepulcher, a tomb that nobody had ever been laid in before (John 19:41RSV Catholic Edition). After three days, he was resurrected from the dead. A virginal birth through Mary to a virginal tomb for rebirth and resurrection.

There are many more stories about the life of Jesus and the ancients of the Bible that refresh the old in the new. We see our Blessed Mother, the Virgin Mary, bringing our Lord into the world in the past. Would it be too presumptuous of us to think that she will bring him into the world again in the second coming of Christ? Saint Louis de Montfort thought so. He wrote about it in his book, *True Devotion to The Blessed Virgin Mary Saint Luis De Montfort, Montfort Publications,1984*. It's not hard to accept this prediction, given the past evidence. We can see clearly a pattern in God's work, and if the devil is the embodiment of the sin of pride, then the lively virtue to combat pride is humility, embodied by the Virgin Mary. Then who might we presume to battle the devil in the end (Revelation 12:1 RSV Catholic Edition)? Coming to know our lady's key role in the life of Jesus and yours will open the door to your mother's love. While we see our original mother of creation, Eve, saying no to God's commands and rebelling, we see our new mother of creation saying yes to God and loving him in obedience. Through Eve, humanity was lost, but through Mary, humanity was saved. Adam, the first man, was led astray by Eve and brought sin and death into our world, inheriting death from him. Jesus, on the other hand, brought life back into the world and conquered death by his perfect atonement for our sins, and through him we inherit life everlasting (John 3:16 RSV Catholic Edition). Through one-man humanity was lost, and through another man humanity was saved. We must honor both our Father and our Mother (Exodus 20:12 RSV Catholic Edition), Jesus (the new Adam), and Mary (the new Eve). Where Jesus is humble, forgiving, and merciful, Mary is gentle, sweet, and encouraging.

When your father presents a job for you to do that seems too difficult to accomplish, you may get discouraged. That's when your mother will encourage you and try to get you everything you need to accomplish your task. Saint Louis de Montfort called Mary the mold that makes everyone like Christ. "With her you become like him much faster than by other means" (*True Devotion to the Blessed Virgin Mary, Saint Luis De Montfort, Montfort Publications,6/1/1984*). Our Blessed Mother is the highest of all the saints, the Queen of Heaven (Revelation 12:1 RSV Catholic Edition). We also see in Genesis 3:15 RSV Catholic Edition where God puts enmity (a rivalry) between Satan and Eve, between her seed and his seed. Who is Mary but none other than the new Eve? Who are her children if not all those who are of the mystical body of Christ? For she gave birth to Christ, and we are his mystical body. So, she gave birth to us as well. Otherwise, she would have only given birth to the head alone, which is Jesus, and a child would not be born without his body (True *Devotion to The Blessed Virgin Mary, Saint Luis De Montfort, Montfort Publications,6/1/1984*).

Then who are the seeds of Satan if not all those who do not believe, do not adore, and do not love God—all those who rebel and do not trust in the sacraments and rules of God's holy church and the commands of our creator in heaven, or in the respect of his pure mother. They are his seed, as once many of us all were, rebelling against God as Lucifer did so long ago and continues to do today. If only they would turn back to God with all their hearts, he would forgive them and heal them (2 Chronicles 7:14 RSV Catholic Edition). Satan still constantly tells everyone the same lie he told Eve: "You don't need God to judge your life; you should judge your life for yourself." Ultimately this path leads to condemnation, so we must trust God and follow his lead.

We also see our Blessed Mother's powerful intercession at the wedding feast in Cana. When the stewards of the wedding ran out of wine to serve (John 2:1–11 RSV Catholic Edition), they told Mary, and she informed Jesus, and Jesus responded, "O Woman, what have you to do with me? My hour has not yet come" (John 2:4 RSV Catholic Edition). Jesus would have never disrespected his mother. If he had, he would have broken one of the Ten Commandments—honor thy father and thy mother—which would have meant that Jesus committed a sin. Jesus, however, was perfect and incapable of sin, but he was entirely capable of speaking in parables so those who have ears to hear may understand. Jesus was not disrespecting his mother but was identifying her as the woman in Genesis whom God the Father was speaking of, as well as the woman in Revelation who was standing on the moon, clothed in the sun, and wearing a crown of twelve stars on her head. We can see that Jesus was not ready to reveal himself by performing this small miracle, but because his mother asked him, he did it anyway and turned water into wine for the wedding. She still intercedes for all of us today.

There are so many reasons why we should have a special devotion to the mother of Christ. I am not the only one who thinks so. Every saint who has ever lived and died in the name of our Lord Jesus has had a loving and tender relationship with our Blessed Mother and has trusted in her intercession with her divine Son. I can honestly say that someone does not have an intense devotion to another person unless they have had a personal and joyous experience with that person. Many of the saints who had this intense devotion to Mary did not come out of thin air. Each one of them has his or her own personal testimony to tell of miracles happening in their lives when they asked Mary, the Mother of God, to pray for them. As if that weren't enough, there are hundreds of confirmed apparitions of the Blessed Virgin Mary all over the world. Every time she reveals herself, thousands of believers go to witness the event. Each event is recorded and documented. The Vatican is extensive when investigating a claimed miracle. If all of the scientific evidence is irrefutable, the event is deemed a miracle.

Every time the Virgin Mary appears to us, she brings us messages about future events and warns us about current ones. She teaches us special prayers to help us appease God's anger and tells all people to get baptized, to believe in her Son, Jesus Christ, and to pray the rosary (*The Great Apparitions of Mary, by Ingo Swann, Crossroad classic, October 25, 1996).* Every time she appears, thousands of skeptics and believers go to see her, and many of them who had malformed limbs or incurable diseases, such as cancer, have been miraculously healed. In every location she has appeared, the church has built a basilica to mark the apparition of Mary that appeared there. Many believers take pilgrimages to these places every year, and miraculous healing takes place, especially when the blessed sacrament is present. The Virgin Mary also has appeared to many holy orders and to special friars and nuns, imparting them with some new devotion to her and Jesus. Many times, she has appeared with Jesus. These other forms of devotion generally pertain to the type of holy order to which she has appeared.

There are three devotions that I have taken on, and I strongly advise you to do the same. Never have I felt closer to Jesus than when I come to him through Mary. If you are constantly with Mary and she is constantly with Jesus, where are you but with Jesus. She will be your advocate in dealings and situations that you cannot see and are unaware of. She will defend you at every turn. As the Memorare prayer says, "Remember, O most gracious Virgin Mary, that never was it known that anyone who fled to thy protection, implored thy help, or sought thy intercession was left unaided. Inspired by this confidence, I fly unto thee, O Virgin of virgins, my Mother; to thee do I come, before thee I stand, sinful and sorrowful. O Mother of the Word Incarnate, despise not my petitions, but in thy mercy, hear and answer me."

All three of these devotions have their own promises that she made to anybody who would faithfully receive them. Let me clarify that these are not superstitious items. They are not some type of good-luck charm. They are a symbol between you and her and to others in your life. They are a representation of your promises to her and her promises to you. These are gifts from heaven to aid humankind, directly from the hands of the Mother of God.

The first devotion I use is the miraculous medal. In the year 1830, Saint Catherine Labouré was visited by an apparition of the Virgin Mary, who instructed her that soon she would oversee a great mission for God and would be given grace to complete the task. She was then visited again by our Blessed Mother, who gave her instructions to have a medal struck with the image of the Blessed Mother on it and this prayer around it: "O Mary, conceived without sin, pray for us who have recourse to thee" (Association of the Miraculous Medal). She had said to Saint Catherine that, "all those who wear it, when it is blessed, will receive great graces, especially if they wear it around their neck." Those who repeat the prayer that is around the outside of the medal in faith will be under the special protection of the Mother of God. Graces will be abundantly bestowed upon those who wear it in confidence. You can pick one of these medals up at any Catholic bookstore. Take it to a priest to have it blessed, and trust in your Blessed Mother's powerful intercession with her Son, Jesus. As if this story could not become more miraculous, when Saint Catherine Labouré died, her body became "incorrupt." This means that her body does not rot. There are many incorrupt saints throughout the world. Many of them have been laid to rest in basilicas. They have been placed in glass coffins so anyone can view these miracles and believe in God.

Many of these saints have the same type of stories linked to them. Generally, they always involve the Mother of God. Many of these saints appear to be sleeping and are well over one hundred years old. Several studies have been done on the bodies, but none of them can be explained by modern science (*The Incorruptibles*, by Joan Carroll Cruz, Tan Books publishers, 1977). Each one has been deemed an approved miracle by the Vatican. Many of the bodies give off a sweet-smelling, flower-like aroma. Some scientists have even put lime in the caskets to speed up the decaying process, but to no avail. All the bodies remain unchanged, and some still have a sweet smell.

The second devotion I recommend is the brown scapular, also known as "The Silent Prayer." On July 16 1251 A.D. Saint Simon Stock was visited by an aparition of the Virgin Mary. She said to him, "Take this scapular; it shall be a sign of salvation, a protection in danger, and a pledge of peace.

Whosoever dies wearing this scapular shall not suffer eternal fire" (*History of the Brown Scapular*). There are many testimonies throughout history of the brown scapular, from stopping bullets to calming stormy seas and bringing hundreds of conversions to the witnesses of these events. The brown scapular is truly extraordinary! Our Blessed Mother continued to tell Saint Simon, "Wear the scapular devoutly and perseveringly; it is my garment. To be clothed in it means you are continually thinking of me, and I in turn am thinking of you and helping you to secure eternal life." Such a loving promise from our lady. In the same way that she promises us, we too make promises to her upon our enrollment. The promises include reciting the little office prayer daily, or praying your rosary upon approval from the priest, and leading a life of chastity, depending on your state in life. The brown scapular has many mysterious stories surrounding it. The latest one is of Saint Alphonsus Liguori. Saint Alphonsus had a special devotion to our Lady of Mount Carmel, and while alive, he wore his brown scapular faithfully. Many years after his death his grave was opened. His body and priestly vestments had turned to dust, but his scapular was found perfectly intact. This was incredible because the scapular is made of wool and would have easily fallen apart long ago. Saint Alphonsus Liguori's brown scapular is still miraculously intact and is on exhibition at his monastery in Rome (*History of the Brown Scapular*).

If you decide to take on this devotion, you must take it seriously out of your love and respect for the Mother of God. There is so much that she does for you that you do not see. She will defend you and prepare you to meet her Son to ask him to pardon you and provide atonement for you for life everlasting. She will adorn you in your good works and will dress you in the charity of your life, adding to it her perfect humility. By wearing your scapular, you are reminded of your love for the Mother of God and are placed in her care. Every time you kiss your scapular, you are telling her that you love her and you love Jesus and all that is good, righteous, and holy. Every time you choose not to sin, you stand firm in your promise to her, and in turn she stands firm in her promise to you. If there is something that you have been praying about but you can't seem to get an answer, hold your scapular and ask your Blessed Mother to ask her Son for you. Her intercession is powerful and effective. Jesus loves her and will give her anything she asks for.

I have had many amazing results by coming to Jesus through Mary. Many of the saints knew this also; they knew that by loving Mary, they were loving Jesus in a distinct way. Through Mary, Jesus gives us our grace, and through Mary, we should return our praise. Giving God praise and worship is like bringing Jesus a bowl of ice cream. It's delicious, satisfying, and sweet, but praising Jesus through his mother is like bringing him a sundae. There's a brownie on the bottom, whipped cream, peanuts, hot fudge, and a cherry on top. It's just dressed up a little more special and it's coming from you, by the hands of his mother, whom he loves. Now that's unique praise! Saint Louis de Montfort once said, "Mary in union with the Holy Spirit, still conceives him and brings him forth daily. It's through her alone that the Son distributes his merits and virtues. The Holy Spirit formed Jesus only thr4ough her, aned he forms the members of his mystical body and dispenses his gifts and favors through her" (True Devotion To The Blessed Virgin Mary, Saint Luis De Montfort, Montfort Press) By coming to know our Lord's Blessed Mother, she then becomes our mother. By keeping a loving devotion to her, we may attain anything that she may bring to Jesus through her powerful intercession and love. For if we love Mary and appreciate her as the Mother of God, the highest of all saints, the

Queen of the Angels, the Mother of Creation (Eve incarnate), and the mother of our hearts, she will always care for our every need. A prayer coming from you is good indeed, but a prayer coming from Mary is humble and irrefutable. Here are what some of the saints have said about the graces we receive from Jesus through her hands:

> "Mary has two sons, the one a God-man, the other mere man. She is the mother first corporally and of the second spiritually." —Saint Bonaventure and Origen

> "This is the will of God who willed that we should have all things through Mary. If then we possess any hope or grace or gift of salvation, let us acknowledge that it comes to us through her." —Saint Bernard

> "All the gifts, graces, and virtues of the Holy Spirit are distributed by the hands of Mary, to whom she wills." —Saint Bernard

> "As you were not worthy that anything divine should be given to you, all graces were given to Mary, so that you might receive through her all graces you would not otherwise receive." —Saint Bernard

> (All quotes from True Devotion To The Blessed Virgin Mary by Saint Luis De Montfort)

Each of the statements above were made by people who were deemed saints by the Catholic church. That means that each one has had at least two incredible healing miracles happen for people who had asked for the intercession of said person. With such devout men and women that close to God, we should seriously consider what teachings and opinions they may have regarding the Mother of God and her relationship with her Son, Jesus Christ, as well as the type of relationship we can have with her so she may lead us in the ways of her divine Son to help us attain eternal consolation and joy. By coming to Jesus through Mary, we ask for her intercession in the same way that the stewards asked for her to intercede for them with Jesus at the wedding feast in Cana. Just like at the wedding feast, whatever she may ask of her Son, he may not be ready to do, but because his mother asks it of him, he just might do it anyway.

The third devotion I recommend is the Mother of Sorrows chaplet. In Saint Alphonsus Liguori's book *The Glories of Mary*, there is mention of a revelation in which Saint John the Evangelist saw both our Lord and his Blessed Mother after her assumption into heaven. He heard Mary ask Jesus for some special grace for all those who were devoted to her dolor's (sorrows). Jesus promised these four special graces to all souls who were devout to this chaplet:

1. That those who, before death, invoked the divine mother in the name of her sorrows should obtain true repentance of their sins.
2. That he would protect all who have this devotion in their tribulations and that he would protect them especially at their death.
3. That he would impress upon their minds the remembrance of his passion and that they should have their reward for it in heaven.

4. That he would commit such devout clients to the hands of Mary with the power to dispose of them in whatever manner she might please, and to obtain for them all the graces she might desire.

Our Blessed Mother made promises to Saint Bridget of Sweden (1303–1373) as well for all those who recite this chaplet daily (De Maria Numquam Satis Amoris).

1. I will grant peace to their families.
2. They will be enlightened about the divine mysteries.
3. I will console them in their pains, and I will accompany them in their work.
4. I will give them as much as they ask for as long as it does not oppose the adorable will of my divine Son or the sanctification of their souls.
5. I will defend them in their spiritual battles with the infernal enemy, and I will protect them at every instant of their lives.
6. I will visibly help them at the moment of their death. They will see the face of their mother.
7. I have obtained this grace from my divine Son that those who propagate this devotion to my tears and dolors will be taken directly from this earthly life to eternal happiness, since all of their sins will be forgiven and my Son will be their eternal consolation and joy.

This powerful devotional chaplet has brought me newfound insight into the divine mysteries. The Mother of Sorrows chaplet gives you our Blessed Mother's perspective on our Lord's bitter passion. As you meditate on Mary's sorrows, your consciousness is swept away and immersed in the setting of each mystery. I will give you one example: When meditating on the sorrow of Jesus carrying the cross, your mind is transported to the streets of Jerusalem, where Jesus carried the cross for us. You can hear the horses' hooves on the ground and the shouts and insults of the crowd as they threw rocks at him and spit at him. You can hear the lashings of the whips from the guards as they constantly beat him to force him to keep moving to Golgotha. The dirt from the street fills your nostrils, and the hot desert sun beats down on your face, and then you witness our Blessed Mother run to her Son and embrace him one last time before he is crucified for us.

This is just one of the mysteries of this chaplet, and there are seven to experience. Each of these dolors humbles you and gives you great reverence for what both Jesus and Mary went through because of us. In turn, we gain great remorse for our sins and great compassion for our Savior and our Blessed Mother. By immersing yourself in her great emotional pain, you allow yourself to connect with her on a level that you never would have known without meditating on these mysteries. By using this chaplet, you are telling her, "I am grateful for your Son, Jesus, and his sacrifice for me, and I will comfort you in your pains as you have comforted me in mine." This degree of reverence and love can only come from two people who comfort each other in mourning after a loved one dies. They support each other and hold one another up so the other may stand firm in whatever has been set before them. Whatever pains and trials may come, they will be nothing compared to the pains you have already been disciplined in by the Queen of Heaven. This fervent love for the Mother of God shows what love you have for our Lord, by connecting with him not just through his bitter passion from the sorrowful mysteries of the most holy rosary, but also through his mother's emotional sorrows by praying this chaplet. Many of us have dealt with heartbreak in our lives, whether it be from a broken relationship, the death of a loved one, or the death of your own child.

Dealing with emotional pain is very hard to work through. If I had a choice, I would choose physical pain over emotional pain any day. To know that the Blessed Mother endured all of that and then continued through her life serving God and nurturing each of the disciples is nothing less than true bravery and strength. She came to think of the disciples as her own children and then had to mourn for them as each one of them was martyred, except for John. If you ever think that what you are dealing with in your life is just too much, set your eyes on Jesus through Mary to find courage in your suffering. As Jesus brings us to repentance (Luke 5:32 RSV Catholic Edition), Mary guides us through that repentance, bestowing on us special strengths and graces, all tailored to our individual needs.

Saint Bonaventure once said this about our Blessed Mother, the Star of the Sea: "Now we must consider how Mary is interpreted 'Star of the Sea.' This name is most suitable to Mary, for she fulfills the office that a star does to mariners at sea. We read, and it is true, that sailors, when they propose to sail to some distant land, choose a star by whose guiding light they may, without going astray, make their way to the land of their desire. Such is certainly the office of Mary, our Star, who directs those who sail through the sea of the world in the ship of the innocence or penance, to the shore of the heavenly country. Well, therefore, doth Innocent say: 'By what aids can ships pass among so many dangers to the shore of the fatherland?' 'Certainly,' he replies, 'chiefly by two. By the wood and by the star; that is, by faith in the Cross, and by virtue of the light which Mary, the Star of the sea, hath brought forth for us. Very properly is Mary compared to a star of the sea, because of her purity, her radiance, and her utility. For Mary is a most pure star, a most radiant star, and a most useful star. She is a most pure star by living most purely; a most radiant star by bringing forth eternal light; a most useful star by directing us to the shores of our true home country" (*Mirror of the Blessed Virgin Mary*, by Saint Bonaventure).

When we allow our Blessed Mother into our repentance, she will help guide us in the ways of her Son. She will prepare you and put her holy approval on you, just as Rebecca prepared Jacob to be blessed by Isaac in the story of Jacob and Esau (Genesis 25:19–34 RSV Catholic Edition). She will defend you when you least expect it and console you in all your sorrows. She will encourage you to seek out piety because through her is the best way to ask Jesus what your mission is. Then she will get you all the graces that you need to accomplish that mission. By staying close to the Mother of God, there is nothing that you cannot ask of Jesus through her. Mary is the closest to our King, and she will prepare whatever is to be set before him to be fit for a king. To be clothed in his mother's humility and to be standing before Jesus wearing such a garment reflects his mother's love for you. To see you having the same deep love he has for his mother gives Jesus a special place in his heart for you. Ask her for help, recommend yourself to her, and honor her sorrows daily to gain reverence and respect for Jesus through Mary, so all the days of your life you may be sheltered by her, defended by her, and adorned by her. Then you will be a soul that is readily prepared to stand before the King of heaven and earth.

Recap: Mary is the highest of all saints, the Queen of Heaven and Mother of Creation. It was through her that our salvation came through to the world, and it is still through her that graces flow to us to aid us in our mission. Our praise can be returned through her to Jesus and be laid at his feet by the hands of his loving mother. All devotions to her, based off our free will, allow her to aid us in our quest to become brothers and sisters of Christ. She will work hard behind the scenes to help you attain eternal life with Jesus. Therefore, you must work hard in life to bring many to her Son, by means of her elegant hands.

Step 10: Have a deeper appreciation for the Mother of God, take on some devotions to her, and ask Jesus if she may help you in your life to help prepare you for your judgment. Continue to research facts about our Blessed Mother. The more you find, the more you will trust in her intercession. Use your devotions in faith and in confidence. She is your mother and mine as well, for we are Christ's body and she gave birth to Christ. Write a letter to the Mother of God, now that you understand that she is your mother too. Impart to her that you love her and didn't know who she was before now. Ask her to come into your life to help you to make Jesus happy. Ask her to pray for you to receive unique gifts personally tailored to your abilities. The Mother of God will never let you down. Take your letter to your parish and read it to her; you may leave the letter with a rose or a flower, acknowledging your great reverence and love for her.

Sign of the cross
O most Blessed Virgin Mary, Mother of Jesus, Mother of Creation, and mother of my heart. I come to thee in confidence and trust in your Son, Jesus Christ, and in you, my queen. I implore you for your assistance, guidance, and

protection throughout my entire life. All my efforts and strides are nothing compared to the achievements that I can accomplish by the grace of God through the means of your holy hands. Please find a special place for me in your immaculate heart. I give you permission to prepare my soul for the day of my death and the moment I stand before your Son at my judgment. I beg you, adorn me in your humility in that very hour and please defend me for the salvation and sanctification of my soul.

Pray for me, O Holy Mother of God, that I may be made worthy of the promises of Christ.

In Jesus's name, amen.

Letter to the Mother of God

Go Forth

NOW THAT YOU have a better understanding of who the Virgin Mary is and the role she plays in God's plan and in our lives, you can humbly ask Jesus for much more help through the hands of his loving mother. Now that we can see Jesus through the eyes and heart of our Blessed Mother, it's time to be closer to Jesus than ever before in the Eucharist. Partaking in the Eucharist is the source and summit of the Christian life (*Catechism of the Catholic Church*). Jesus renews our spirit, heals us, and allows us to partake in his peace, which rests on each one of us when we partake in Holy Communion with him. When we consume the Eucharist, we consume the physical body and blood of Jesus Christ. By the consecration of the priest, the physical state of nthe bread and the winechange to the body and blood of our Lord Jesus Christ, as I discussed earlier in the chapter, "Words Are Powerful". When you consume the body and blood of Christ, the spirit of Jesus dwells within you. Partaking in the Eucharist regularly keeps you within the great mystical body of Christ. It is as near to Jesus as we can possibly get while still here on earth. Jesus said to those he was teaching in John 6:56 RSV Catholic Edition, "Whoever eats my flesh and drinks my blood remains in me and I in them." To remain in the great body of Christ makes us one of his appendages, constantly reaching out to others to reflect Christ's love in this world that is full of sadness and pain.

Saint Paul calls the great body of Christ's holy church to be dependent on one another as your feet are dependent on your hands, your nose to your mouth, and so on and so forth (1 Corinthians 12 RSV Catholic Edition). Do you remember what Jesus said to the crowd after raising Lazarus from the dead? Lazarus came out of the tomb wrapped in his grave clothes (representing sin), and Jesus said to the community standing around him, "Unbind him and let him go " (John 11:44 RSV Catholic Edition). This means that Jesus wants us to not only rely on him but also to rely on his mystical body of believers to help one another, therefore, being each an appendage in Christ's body. We are called to participate in his work, to untie each other from our sin, as well as continue the message of our Lord's holy gospel to the world. If it is true then that we are all connected in the great mystical body to Jesus and to each other, doesn't that mean that we are connected to all saints in heaven also? They especially are in the great mystical body and are alive, enjoying eternal life.

Just as all the appendages are dependent on one another here on earth, they too are dependent on us and we are dependent on them. This interaction between the saints in heaven and our friends and relatives who have passed away and all of us who are living is called the communion of saints. We are the church militant, they are the church triumphant, and our relatives if in purgatory are the church suffering (*Catechism of the Catholic Church*, page 249). Seeing as we are all connected in the great mystical body, we can easily ask the saints in heaven to ask our Lord for some extra help in our lives. Always remember, you were created to do God's will. When we are seeking to do the will of God, we can ask Jesus for all that we need to complete our mission. We can also ask him to appoint us specific saints to correspond with us on whatever mission we have been appointed to accomplish or whatever situation we are dealing with that would pertain to the life of a specific saint. Jesus will give you all that you ask, especially if he's asked for you by some of his dearest friends.

When you were baptized, you made promises to God and to the church, and when you became confirmed, you affirmed these beliefs. The promises you made at baptism are as follows:

1. Do you reject Satan?
2. And all his works?
3. And all his empty promises?
4. Do you believe in God the Father Almighty, the Creator of heaven and earth?
5. Do you believe in Jesus Christ, his only Son, our Lord, who was born of the Virgin Mary, was crucified, died and was buried, rose from the dead, and is now seated at the right hand of the Father?
6. Do you believe in the Holy Spirit, the holy Catholic church, the communion of saints, the forgiveness of sins, the resurrection of the body, and life everlasting?
7. God, the all-powerful Father of our Lord, Jesus Christ has given us a new birth by water and the Holy Spirit, and forgiven all our sins. May he also keep us faithful to our Lord, Jesus Christ, forever and ever, amen.

These promises are now confirmed in confirmation, where you stand in front of your community and agree to all the promises you made during your baptism. Once you have received the sacrament of confirmation, you are more perfectly bound to Jesus and the church, which is the mystical body. It is the closing end of your baptism. In doing this you are enriched with extraordinary gifts and strengths of the Holy Spirit. Hence you become a true witness of Christ, more strictly obliged to spread and defend the Christian faith by word and deed (*Catechism*, page 326). For you to be able to defend the faith, you will have to tap into the gifts given to you by the Holy Spirit, which you will receive after you have been anointed with the chrism oil by the priest. Now you belong to Jesus; this anointing of oil puts our Lord's seal on you and strengthens our baptismal grace. By receiving our Lord's seal, you also receive the Holy Spirit (*Catechism*, page 328). When you are anointed with the chrism oil, you are being anointed with oil that the bishop and the entire dioceses of priests have invoked the Holy Spirit to enter. You not only are getting anointed by the oil, but you are also getting anointed with gladness, clothing with light, a cloak of salvation, a spiritual gift, the sanctification of souls and bodies, imperishable happiness, the indelible seal, a buckler of faith, and a fearsome helmet against all the works of the adversary (*Catechism*, page 329). Then the bishop or priest will extend his hands over you and the congregation using the same gesture as the disciples did, which represents the giving of the Holy Spirit. The Holy Spirit is then invoked by reciting this prayer:

> "All-Powerful God, Father of our Lord, Jesus Christ, by water and the Holy Spirit you freed your sons and daughters from sin and gave them new life. Send your Holy Spirit upon them to be their helper and guide. Give them the spirit of wisdom and understanding, the spirit of right judgment and courage, the spirit of

knowledge and reverence. Fill them with the spirit of wonder and awe in your presence. We ask this through Christ, our Lord" (*Catechism*, page 329).

The Holy Spirit will then come alive in you and will awaken your spiritual gifts. These gifts that you received or will receive at your confirmation are as follows:

Wisdom: The gift of wisdom is our ability to value spiritual things over worldly ones. It enables us to desire the things of God and correctly order the things in our life. This gift helps us view the world through God's perspective and the light of our faith. It instills a desire to contemplate the things of God.

Understanding: This helps us grasp the truths of faith more easily and profoundly. Our human intellect cannot grasp all of God's mysteries, but through the gift of understanding, we can be led to truth, even when we do not fully comprehend God's awesome power. This gift strengthens our insight through prayer, scripture, and sacraments.

Counsel: The gift of counsel acknowledges the difference between right and wrong and bestows proper judgment. A person with the right judgment avoids sin and leads a life for Christ. Counsel inspires us to speak up and encourage others to do the right thing. It bestows upon us prudence, allowing us to act promptly and rightly in the face of difficult situations.

Courage: This gift sustains our decision to follow the will of God in any situation. It allows us to stand up and defend our faith even when threatened by bodily injury or death. Courage allows us to be steadfast in our decisions to dwell and to endure evil, even when we do not want to.

Knowledge: This is an awareness of God's plan. It is not simply an accumulation of facts, but rather an understanding of God's purpose and how we ought to respond. Knowledge helps bring to light the temptations we face and to discern whether to give in or live a life worthy of God's approval.

Piety: Piety or reverence is our obedience to God and our willingness to serve him. It is not just obedience through a sense of duty or obligation, but rather obedience out of love and devotion. It facilitates a deeper respect and honor for God and his church.

Wonder and Awe: This gift makes us aware of the glory and majesty of God. It is synonymous with "the fear of the Lord," in which we dread sin and fear of offending God. We fear displeasing God and losing our connection with him because of our love for him. Wonder and awe increase our desire to draw closer to God and to depart from sin.

(All explanations of spiritual gifts are quoted from the catholic company.com)

We know that we receive these gifts because of the events that took place in the life of Jesus. First, when he was baptized by John the Baptist in the Jordan River, Jesus came out of the water and the Spirit of the Lord came down from heaven and rested on Jesus (Matthew 3:16 RSV Catholic Edition), and second, when Jesus came back to life through the resurrection at Easter, he came to his disciples, extended his hands, and said, "Receive the Holy Spirit" (John 20:22 RSV Catholic Edition). Jesus passed these gifts of the Holy Spirit to his disciples and the disciples to their priests and so on to our priests today and from our priests to us. The prophet Isaiah even prophesized about these gifts of the Holy Spirit in Isaiah 11:2–3 RSV Catholic Edition: "The Spirit of the Lord shall rest upon him. The spirit of wisdom and understanding, the spirit of counsel and might, the spirit of knowledge and the fear of the Lord."

All of us are born with specific talents and skills that are given to us by God, and we are expected to use these skills and talents to contribute to God's plan of saving humankind. After you become confirmed, your hidden spiritual gifts will be revealed to you to also contribute to your greater fortitude toward the good works of God—to bear fruit, to help gather with Jesus all those who are willing to be saved. Jesus once told a parable of the three servants in Mathew 25:14-30 RSV Catholic Edition. He said, "For it will be as when a man going on a journey called his servants and entrusted to them his property; to one he gave five talents, to another two, to another one, to each according to his ability. Then he went away. He who had received the five talents went at once and traded with them; and he made five talents more. So also, he who had two talents made two talents more. But he who had received the one talent went and dug in the ground and hid his master's money. Now after a long time the master of those servants came and settled accounts with them. And he wo received the five talents came forward, bringing five talents more, saying, Master, you delivered to me five talents here I have made five talents more.' His master said to him. 'Well done, good and faithful servant; you have been faithful over a little, I will set you over much; enter into the joy of your master.' And he also who had two talents came forward saying, Master, you delivered to me two talents; here I have made two talents more.' His master said to him, 'well done good and faithful servant; you have been faithful over a little, I will set you over much; enter into the joy of your master. He also who had received the one talent came forward, saying, 'Master I knew you to be a hard man, reaping where you did not sow, and gathering where you did not winnow; so, I was afraid, I went and hid your talent in the ground here have what is yours.' But his master answered him, you wicked and slothful servant! You Knew that I reap where I have not sowed, and gather where I have not winnowed? Then you ought to Have invested my money with the bankers, and at my coming I should have received what was my own with interest. So, take the talent from him, and give it to him who has the ten talents. For to everyone who has will more be given, and he will have an abundance; but from him who has not, even what he has will be taken away. And cast the worthless servant into the outer darkness; there men will weep and gnash their teeth.'"

Jesus is telling us here that we are all given gifts and he expects us to produce with what gifts he has given us. If we do absolutely nothing and do not serve him in any way whatsoever, I don't think he will be too happy. Jesus said, "He who is not with me is against me and he who does not gather with me scatters (Matthew 12:30 RSV Catholic Edition). Have you ever heard someone say all roads lead to heaven? Is that person gathering with Jesus or scattering abroad? Jesus said there is only one road that leads to heaven, and that road is through him (John 14:6 RSV Catholic Edition). Therefore, the gospel was created to gather all of those who would believe in Jesus and would repent, turning from their sin to a merciful Creator who came to save what was lost (Luke 19:10 RSV Catholic Edition). For he has mercy on those who love him, Romans 8:28 Catholic Edition says, "we know that in everything, God works for good with those who love him, who are called according to his purpose."

You are being called now. Will you love God or go back to other worldly living? Will you turn a profit from the gifts he gave you? Or will you bury his gifts in the ground and do nothing? Jesus once told the parable of the vine and the branches (John 15:1-17 RSV Catholic Edition). Jesus said, "I am the true vine, and my Father is the vinedresser. Every branch of mine that bears no fruit, he takes away, and every branch that does bear fruit he prunes, that it may bear more fruit. You are already made clean by the word which I have spoken to you. Abide in me, and I in you. as the branch cannot bear fruit by itself, unless it abides in the vine, neither can you unless you abide in me. I am the vine, you are the branches he who abides in me, and I in him, he it is that bears much fruit, for apart from me you can do nothing. If a man does not abide in me, he is cast fourth as a branch and withers; and the branches are gathered, thrown into the fire and burned. If you abide in me and my words abide in you ask whatever you will and it shall be done for you. By this my Father is glorified, that you bear much fruit, and so prove to be my disciples. As the Father has loved me, so have I loved you; abide in my love. If you keep my commandments, you will abide in my love, just as I have kept my Father's commandments and abide in his love. These things I have spoken to you, that my joy may be in you, and that your joy may be full. This is my commandment that you love one another as I have loved you. Greater love has no man than this, that a man lay down his life for his friends. You are my friends if you do what I command you. No longer do I call you servants, for the servant does not know what his master is doing; but I have called you friends, for all that I have heard from my Father I have made known to you. You did not choose me, but I chose you and appointed you that you should go and bear fruit and that your fruit should abide; so that whatever you ask the Father in my name, he may give it to you. This I command you, to love one another."

Matthew 7:18-20 RSV Catholic Edition also says, "So, every sound tree bears good fruit, but the bad tree bears evil fruit, a sound tree cannot bear evil fruit, nor can a bad tree bear good fruit. Every tree that does not bear good fruit is cut down and thrown into the fire. Thus, you will know them by their fruits." We must bear fruit for God, and we must accomplish our mission, all while staying attached to the vine, which is Jesus. We must partake in the Eucharist to stay in Jesus and for Jesus to stay in us, and for us to partake in the Eucharist, we must go to confession, trying evermore to avoid the near occasion of sin so we can be a good tree that bears good fruit instead of a bad tree that cannot.

Now you are fully equipped for your mission, with all the spiritual gifts and talents you need to work diligently toward producing fruit, saving souls, and continuing to share the gospel of Jesus Christ. Saint Paul once said, " Though I am free and belong to no one, I have made myself a slave to everyone, to win as many as I can" (1Corinthians 9:19 RSV Catholic Edition). So pray your rosary and your Mother of

Sorrows chaplet, and read scripture and good works that the saints have produced to aid us and our Lord in gathering as many as we can. Be brave and courageous, speaking boldly of our Lord when evangelizing and defending the faith, for you are with him, not against him. So take your gifts, pursue your mission with zeal, and go forth.

Recap: You made God a promise at baptism, when you received your special graces from God. At your confirmation, these gifts will become known to you. You must believe in faith when you receive this sacrament to fully understand your gifts. Your gifts are meant to help God gather all that he can for the kingdom of heaven and to help your brothers and sisters with their sin. Jesus is the vine and we are the branches. If we are expected to bear fruit with our gifts, we must stay on the vine. Keeping our Lord's commandments and receiving communion honestly by attending reconciliation will keep you attached to Jesus so you may bear much fruit.

Step 11: Kneel before the tabernacle and ask Jesus what he would like you to do. Offer him praise and thanksgiving through his mother's immaculate heart to show him that you are grateful for the gifts he has given you and you are ready for your mission. Ask him to reveal your next step, and don't just ask, sit and listen. Write down any ideas you may have in that moment. Jesus may not give you an answer right away. We're on God's time, not ours. Keep persistently asking until you have an idea of what he wants you to do. This may take several separate occasions of asking. I highly recommend praying your rosary before the tabernacle and tasking each time.

In doing this you will be asking Jesus through his mother's immaculate heart.

Sign of the cross
O most merciful Jesus, I thank you for bringing me all this way. I didn't know who I was before I came to you, and now you have shown me who I can be. Please continue to mold me, to shape me into your image. Please make my life be meaningful to you. I wish to serve you, to do your will, and to do penance to amend my life. I humbly ask for some work to do for you. Please entrust me with some responsibilities so I may prove helpful to you and to the kingdom of heaven. Now that I am in your grace, please help me remain there all my life. I give myself entirely to you as did all the saints who came before me. Please send me where you must, instruct me on where to go, and transform me from ordinary to extraordinary.

In your name, Lord, this I pray, amen.

What Is Jesus Asking of You?

The Beginning

I FIND IT fascinating that where this journey ends a new one begins. Use all the knowledge contained in this book to continue to serve our Lord, Jesus Christ. Ask your Blessed Mother for help and Blessed Saint Joseph, her spouse, and all the saints in heaven. Even ask your grandmother or grandfather who has passed away for help. Their prayers matter too. Stay close to Jesus through his mother's immaculate heart. Spend time with him daily in prayer. Pray the rosary and the Mother of Sorrows chaplet daily to allow our Blessed Mother to mold you into the perfect image of her Son. Wear your scapular for protection. You're going to need it once you start bearing fruit to bring others to Jesus. Come to Jesus for counsel when making big decisions. Avoid the near occasion of sin and live a God-centered life.

If you keep God at the center of your life, he will properly align everything else in your life for you in accordance with his will because, ultimately, the goal is to spend an eternity with him in heaven. That's why we need him to show us the road and how to get there. Use God's holy church and the family of believers to help you with your sin and your good works. Go to confession regularly, go to Mass every Sunday, and consume the Eucharist to remain in the great mystical body of our Lord, Jesus Christ. Be charitable and have compassion for the less fortunate. *Love one another as Christ loved you*. Be tender and kind to each other, forgive everyone, and hold no grudges. Let God's guiding light show you where to go. Trust in our merciful Savior even in the face of danger. Defend the faith even in the face of death. Be courageous and brave, steadfast and strong. Do not fear the devil; the devil should fear you! Good luck on your mission. Fulfill your purpose so God may fulfill his promises to you, for our faith is a faith of action and hard work, not just by grace alone but by good deeds as well (James 2:22 RSV Catholic Edition). The hope of God is the salvation of all men. So, let's all give him a reason to mold us into a new creation and convert us from the ordinary people we used to be to the extraordinary people we were born to be.

Anybody Can Become a Saint

You don't have to be a priest or a nun to become a saint. Below is a list of saints; only a few eventually joined a holy order, but this wasn't until much later in their life. Most of these saints were just good Christians, were married, and did not join any holy orders. I want to emphasize this because the body of Christ is so large and our priests are so few. If you feel a calling to religious life, please consider that path. If not, just know that we are all called to do God's work. We are all called to love, and we are all called to become saints.

(Search for these saints online. It takes five minutes to get inspired by their incredible virtue.)

- Saint Gianna Beretta Molla (married, physician, children)
- Saint George of England (soldier)
- Saints Nereus and Achilleus, (brothers, soldiers)
- Saint Maria Goretti
- Saint Agatha of Sicily
- Saint Martha of Bethany
- Saint Ursula (princess)
- Saint Kateri Tekakwitha
- Saint Abigail
- Saint Anastasia
- Saint Barbara
- Saint Juan Diego
- Saint Catherine of Alexandria
- Saint Elizabeth of Hungary (married)
- Saint Margaret of Scotland
- Saint Jerome
- Saint Lorenzo Ruiz (married)
- Saint Philomena
- Saint Christina

- Saints Joachim and Anne (married, parents of our Blessed Mother)
- Saint James the Greater, Apostle
- Saint James the Less, Apostle
- Saint Mark, Apostle
- Saint Thomas, Apostle
- Saint Matthew, Apostle
- Saint John, Apostle
- Saint Luke, Apostle
- Saint Peter, Apostle
- Saint Jude, Apostle
- Saint Paul, Apostle
- Saint Andrew, Apostle
- Saint Joseph (stepfather of Jesus)
- Saint Mary (Mother of Jesus and mother of us all)
- Saint Joan of Arc (soldier)
- Saint Sebastian (soldier)
- Saint Agnes
- Saint Lucy
- Saint Cecilia (first incorrupt saint)
- Saint Elizabeth
- Saint Dominic Savio

I am not capable of doing big things,
But I want to do everything,
Even the smallest things,
For the greater glory of God.

—Saint Dominic Savio

We look not on your sins
But what you were destined to do
Before your life began

—Saint Michael the Archangel

Our Hearts

It is with our hearts
That we love
that we honor
that we trust
that we forgive
that we pardon
that we believe
that we have faith
and that we promise.
Therefore, let us not be led away
To the corruption of our hearts
by lying
by coveting
by our broken promises
by our deceit
by our disloyalty
and by our desires

and let not the desires of our hearts
lead us into temptation
and let not our weakness
be overcome
when tempted
pushing us over the line
from temptation
into sin.

—Jerad Bisson

CPSIA information can be obtained
at www.ICGtesting.com
Printed in the USA
FSOW02n1940080118
43191FS